MW00335049

the WOMEN'S
BOOKSHOP
105 Ponsonby Rd, Auckland
Ph: (09) 376 4399
books@womensbookshop.co.nz

ROCK
AROUND THE KITCHEN

fresh, funky food that happens
to be good for you

**PETER CHAPLIN
& MARY COX**

**PHOTOGRAPHS BY
SHAUN CATO-SYMONDS**

RANDOM HOUSE
NEW ZEALAND

dedication

To the memory of Thomas MacPherson Chaplin,
for love, for guidance and for bringing us to New Zealand; Peter

For my mother, my grandmother and my daughter; Mary

acknowledgements

Thanks to: Bhana Bros, Ponsonby Road, Auckland; Marisa Jelas and Karl at Mt Eden
Fisheries, Dominion Road, Auckland; Spicewise, Auckland; The Tofu Shop, Dominion Road,
Auckland; Noel Quinlivan at The Clare Inn, Dominion Road, Auckland; Breville NZ Limited;
and the team at TVNZ's *Good Morning* show.

BLUMENFELD
OLIVE OIL LIMITED
NEW ZEALAND

www.blumenfeld.co.nz

Blumenfeld, "the Champagne of Olive Oil", is a product of the late Gidon Blumenfeld,
pioneer of the commercial olive oil industry in New Zealand. I discovered this fine extra
virgin oil while presenting at the Marlborough Wine and Food Festival in New Zealand.

I am seriously addicted to Blumenfeld Olive Oil and it is my preferred olive oil for all
the recipes in this book. I have used the oil religiously during my cooking segments on
TVNZ's *Good Morning* show for the past two years and continue to drizzle and cook with it,
for its flavour and good health, wherever I go.

Peter Chaplin

No information in this book constitutes a prescription or advice for any specific ailment. If you have a
medical problem, consult a qualified medical practitioner. If you are prone to allergic reactions, patch-test
ingredients. Check properties of herbs and essential oils: some are unsuitable for use during pregnancy.

National Library of New Zealand Cataloguing-in-Publication Data

Chaplin, Peter.
Rock around the kitchen : fresh, funky food that happens to be good for you
/ Peter Chaplin, Mary Cox.
Includes index.
ISBN 1-86941-639-2
1. Cookery. I. Cox, Mary, 1951- II. Title.
641.563—dc 22

A RANDOM HOUSE BOOK
published by
Random House New Zealand
18 Poland Road, Glenfield, Auckland, New Zealand
www.randomhouse.co.nz

First published 2004

© 2004 text: Peter Chaplin and Mary Cox; photography: Shaun Cato-Symonds
The moral rights of the authors have been asserted

ISBN 1 86941 639 2

Cover and text design: Nick Turzynski
Printed in China

contents

introducing
peter chaplin

I love food, I have always loved food, and I will forever love food! Food is almost like a second skin for me. It represents my professional journey and my artistic pursuit as a chef and a restaurateur. Food acts as my messenger, seeking to inform and educate others about the benefits of good food and good health. As a restaurateur, I have found it my absolute joy to provide plates of food to eagerly awaiting 'souls' in need of nourishment. There is something primal and ancient in the satisfaction of giving and receiving good food.

Music has been a major motivator and a huge influence in my life. Music, like food, fuelled my ambition to travel the world to experience different tastes and musical styles. As a Piscean, I find music vitally important to my creative and artistic side. I can remember where and when I first heard a particular piece of music, in exactly the same way a perfume or a culinary aroma can evoke an emotive memory. There is no doubt the musical and social explosion of the '60s had a profound effect on me. It seems quite incredible that in my emerging career as a chef I drove straight into the musical kitchen of the Thompson Twins, Orchestral Manoeuvres In the Dark, The Pretenders, Iggy Pop and Madonna.

My big break came in 1985, when Alannah Currie and Tom Bailey (the Thompson Twins) were looking for a chef who understood the philosophy of vegetarian food, for their upcoming rock 'n' roll world tour. Chrissie Hynde then heard of my culinary prowess and I found myself on another 12-month world tour. Chrissie introduced me to Madonna, who was preparing for a world tour in 1987 and looking for the best vegetarian chef in rock 'n' roll.

As personal chef to Madonna, I was solely responsible for maintaining nutrition levels to ensure that her body had enough fuel to complete a three-hour daily workout and two-hour show, four days a week during her tour. Following this amazing experience I opened my first restaurant, Musical Knives, in Melbourne and developed the Musical Knives Cooking School. In 1990 I was asked to rejoin Madonna on her 'Blond Ambition' tour, a professional accolade indeed. I then returned to Melbourne before moving back to New Zealand in 1992 and re-establishing Musical Knives Restaurant and Cooking School in Ponsonby, Auckland. In 1997, the restaurant was recognised with the inaugural 'Most Innovative Cuisine' award by the New Zealand Restaurant Association. For the last few years I have regularly appeared on TVNZ's *Good Morning* show, presenting healthy, modern vegetarian recipes.

Mary Cox suggested we write a book together and she became the catalyst for my dream to produce a cookbook. I had been aware of a strong desire to pass on my knowledge and enthusiasm for food and cooking to a larger audience. With this book, I hope that I can encourage you to have confidence to take control in the kitchen — but most of all I want to show that you can enjoy cooking my style of food *and* benefit from it as well. In the restaurant, and through teaching, I have shown people 'the way' with my food. The knowledge and passion I have for my task are worth nothing unless I can pass them on. Like Mary, I never wanted to be a saint. I believe that you can still enjoy coffee, wine, food and sweet desserts so long as you have a good nutritional platform. Let the music play and rock you around the kitchen.

introducing
mary cox

A good deal of my childhood was spent in what, back in the 1950s, were known as 'infectious diseases' hospitals. On one occasion, when I was discharged from hospital, my mother was going through a difficult pregnancy and so my grandmother took over caring for me.

For many years, I carried the 'sickly child' label and was away from school quite a lot, but these were small prices to pay for the knowledge my grandmother passed on to me during the weeks and months I spent in bed after one illness or another. She swore by onions and garlic for their antibiotic properties, leeks for sore throats, fish as food for the soul, and beetroot as a blood cleanser. Cod-liver oil lubricated the insides, and for her water was life's blood because it not only cleansed the body, it could also be used in other forms to pep up the heart, lungs and circulation. I wouldn't say that all of the remedies she concocted tasted good — in fact some of them were downright unpleasant — but we both persevered, and her uncanny knowledge of the health benefits found in herbs, spices, fruits and vegetables paid off for me.

Although I did not realise it then, my bouts of ill health and my grandmother's care helped to shape my life's journey. It is a journey that has seen me study the workings of the human body, the healing power of food, plants, herbs, essential oils, flower essences, colour healing, Chinese philosophies and many other natural therapies. A journey that inspired me to run health and natural rebalance therapy courses and to open a successful beauty and natural therapy training school in Auckland, New Zealand. A journey that gave birth to my first book, *Gravity Sucks or Does It? A common sense approach to loving the body you live in.* A journey that took me into the kitchen of TVNZ's *Good Morning* show, where I enjoy creating lotions and potions for beauty, health and wellbeing, using everyday foods found in the kitchen cupboard, local supermarkets and health-food stores.

Peter and I meet regularly on the set of the *Good Morning* show and rock our way around the studio kitchen. We often use the same ingredients in our respective cooking, health and beauty segments — and so *Rock Around the Kitchen* was born.

Food talks; it shows in your skin, in the brightness of your eyes, the shine on your hair, the way you walk and the shape of your body. *Rock Around the Kitchen* was written to encourage you to take a good look at your diet. It carries the message that you can eat for pleasure and for health at the same time. I have compiled a range of delicious, nutritious juices, found at the end of the book. To complement Peter's recipes, I have focused on specific ingredients with health-giving or other properties and that can be made into simple lotions, potions and old-fashioned remedies.

So go on: give it a go, turn up the music, rock around the kitchen, create these delicious recipes and check out the food for thought and health benefit sections. Make the lotions, potions and old-fashioned remedies in your own kitchen and enjoy life!

peter chaplin: recipes that rock

Over the last 20 years New Zealand has experienced a significant change in culture when it comes to food. With access to a wide variety of foods from all over the world, this country has become very international when it comes to taste and attitude. Kiwis have embraced the 'food wave' and this is reflected in *Rock Around the Kitchen*.

The food I cook is my 'world tour'. My years of travel, soaking up every piece of information, inspiration, taste, texture and aromas of the food from the many different countries I have visited, have resulted in a distinctive style of cooking.

Rock Around the Kitchen is a modern Kiwi cookbook with a variety of recipes from around the world, using fresh food, herbs and spices. The book is broken down into easy, user-friendly sections. Where possible, preparation time has been kept to a minimum, with simplicity being the operative word. It's all about fresh food cooked quickly, for maximum results. Ten minutes is all that is required to slice up vegetables, and five minutes in the wok or pan yield maximum nutritional value.

To create the recipes in your own kitchen you will need a good knife, a zester, juicer, food processor or blender; some pots, pans and a wok; a little bit of organisation; a modest pantry and an appetite for good-quality, nutritious food.

I believe that the three most important sensory factors in cooking good food are **visual** (food looks good), **aroma** (food smells good) and **taste** (food that has texture and tastes good). Satisfaction and nutrition are an added bonus. If the food you cook nourishes and leaves you and your body satisfied, then it is good for you and will bring benefits to your health and wellbeing.

Fresh food and clean taste are the two factors that dominate *Rock Around the Kitchen*. The recipes in this book can be adapted to include meat or chicken if that's your preference. Love and passion are stamped throughout the book and all of the meals have graced the tables of family and friends.

I love definite, bold tastes. I love crisp fresh vegetables, al dente pasta and noodles. My philosophy is to just, and only just, cook the vegetables to create texture and taste. Fresh garlic and ginger — I would not want to live without them. There is a definite clarity to the taste of garlic and ginger: vibrant and stimulating.

Some recipes have a large assortment of vegetables and some a variety of seeds and spices. Do not be too concerned if you are missing the odd one or two. Use what you have readily available in the pantry and fridge. Most of the ingredients listed are available from large supermarkets (see glossary). The others you will find in Asian, Japanese or well-stocked health-food stores.

Some recipes are of classic origin; for example, the flans, desserts and soups. Of the desserts, the Melon and Mint Sorbet is totally nouvelle cuisine in concept and technique, and the Chocolate Cherry Hazelnut Cake is Italian. The Chilled Pear Peppermint Soup with Vanilla is also nouvelle cuisine and the Coconut Pumpkin Dhal Soup is Indian. But I must confess to reinterpreting the classics wildly at times, with surprisingly good results.

Other recipes are completely 'fresh off the boat'. Funky Calamari was an outside bet that became a winner on its first outing during Christmas 2003. Celeriac Fish Soup was developed during a wet summer's day in 2004. Corn thinnies and lettuce rolls burst forth during holidays at the bach on Medlands Beach, Great Barrier Island and at Ocean Beach, on the Whangarei Heads.

The Aubergine and Ricotta Roulade and Doris Plum and Honey Cheesecake are the only recipes that need to be prepared a day ahead. For anyone who's keen to keep preparation time to an absolute minimum, there is a Fast and Furious section, which contains fresh, healthy, quick meals. There are good ideas for barbecues and summer days at the bach. Check out the essential tips for cooking tofu and tempeh and have a go at the rice and noodle dishes.

Soups are really important. They may appear humble but they are often more nutritious than you might expect. Soups are always well received and, like a glass of water, are the sustenance of life. There is a wonderful array of soups to be discovered in this book. The Kumara, Ginger and Coriander Soup is uniquely Kiwi; the Spinach and Parsley Soup is green and traditional; the Roasted Bell Pepper and Tomato Soup is continental Mediterranean; there is classic French in the Courgette and Thyme Soup; and the Pea, Potato and Brewer's Yeast Soup is a fresh concept. Look out for the Chilled Pear Peppermint Soup — delicious, to say the least.

Noodles and pasta are fast, fun, versatile foods. Rice is the staple food of many countries and could be considered the most important grain on the planet. Noodles and pasta need minimal technique and knowledge; they are not at all daunting. These recipes are probably some of the most convenient foods to cook; they are quick and easy to create and a pleasure to serve. The Cashew Basmati Rice, Bergamo Peasant Spaghetti, Sendai Soba Noodles and Roasted Pumpkin and Pine Nut Pasta can be eaten hot or cold.

Seafood is the classic cuisine of New Zealand and we are spoiled with its range, quality and price. The recipes in the seafood section are all stars — recipes that will be greeted with admiration and enthusiasm — but I have to say the monkfish recipe with its fluffy, moist texture is most definitely a superstar. Not far behind is the Japanese-influenced calamari seasoned with wasabi, garlic and cracked black pepper. The use of chickpea flour on the Spiced Terakihi Fillets covers the fish with a beautiful golden-yellow tone and a crispy texture. Smoked New Zealand seafood is in a class of its own. Do try the Smoked Kahawai and Leek Salad with walnuts.

It would be easy for me to say that Vegetable Salads is my favourite section, so I shall. I love the savoury velvet of Balsamic Beetroot, with its liquorice-like texture combined with the sweetness of balsamic vinegar and the added savoury taste of garlic. The Broccoli, Cashew and Marinated Tofu Salad is an Asian–French fusion with the vibrancy of coriander, ginger and lemon, complemented by roasted cashews and crispy blanched broccoli flowerets. I love strong, bold tastes — and the Watercress and Marinated Mushroom Salad does it for me every time. The simplicity of the Peanut Noodle Salad and the chilled rice salad make them old friends at any dinner table.

Iggy Pop and I became good mates during The Pretenders' world tour in 1987. One of Iggy's favourites was the Aubergine and Ricotta Roulade, a chilled roll of seasoned ricotta cheese wrapped in roasted slices of aubergine with garlic, fresh oregano and capers. A real wild child. The Peach and Parmesan Flan is an Italian classic, designed to fuel your imagination with its sweet and savoury combination encased in a seductive short pastry. The Green Bean Frittata is a home favourite and such an adaptable recipe that it can be served regularly. The Florentine and Goat Cheese Tart makes excellent travel or picnic food and is my Boxing Day table standby.

Legumes and grains are a staple in any balanced diet. Minty Couscous with Avocado and Orange Segments, a favourite on Madonna's 'Blond Ambition' tour, is a must-try. The Parsley, Corn and Tomato Polenta is an old savoury Italian favourite. Anyone with wheat or dairy allergies will love the Hazelnut Fritters. The Coconut Chickpea Curry is reminiscent of Genoa and the romance of Italy, while the Black Rice Mushroom Cakes recall hot days and cool nights on Phuket Island off the coast of Thailand.

Everybody loves a star, so be sure to try the Chocolate Cherry Hazelnut Cake; it is without doubt a superstar. The Strawberry Sweethearts and the Doris Plum and Honey Cheesecake are stars of seduction. The Lemon and Pear Flan, the Star Anise Apple Bran Crumble, the Melon and Mint Sorbet and the delicious Cashew and Rhubarb Delight are humble stars, suitable for everyday occasions.

The juices devised by Mary are easy to make and delicious to drink. When time is a pressure, they will provide a quick, healthy boost of nutrition and energy. With 12 different recipes to try, there is a flavour and a style for every palate. The Apple, Orange and Tofu Trio is sweet to taste and very nutritious. The Banana and Lime Frost Zinger will put spring into your step. The Beetroot, Celery and Apple Cleanser will help boost any immune system. Coffee lovers — do check out the Blueberry Latte. For the lactose intolerant, the Rice Milk Smoothie is a perfect breakfast treat. The Green Goddess, full of the natural cleanser chlorophyll, is a useful blood tonic and rich in vitamins and minerals. Juices can be served as appetisers, entrées or as a dessert. They are perfect for breakfast, lunch or dinner. Use your imagination; garnish them with nuts, herbs, fruits or colourful cocktail umbrellas.

Mary's other recipes — for rejuvenating tonics and remedies that have stood the test of time — are an ideal complement for the food. They offer simple, natural ways to freshen up and feel better using everyday ingredients that you'll find in your kitchen cupboard.

A healthy skin, healthy body and healthy mind are three vital components of a happy, well-balanced lifestyle. Believe it or not . . . it all comes down to what you eat and what you drink! Unleash your creative juices, sling your hook, and get out there. All you have to do is source the ingredients and then *Rock Around the Kitchen.*

soups

kumara, ginger and coriander soup

coconut pumpkin dhal soup

roasted bell pepper and
    tomato soup with basil

chilled pear peppermint soup with vanilla

courgette and thyme soup with asparagus

pea, potato and brewer's yeast soup

spinach and parsley soup

kumara, ginger and coriander soup

This 'Kiwi style' soup combines the gorgeous texture of kumara with vibrant spices and refreshing lemon zest. I often refer to this dish as 'my nourishing friend'.

SERVES 8

4 tbsp olive oil
4 medium kumara or sweet potatoes, scrubbed and finely diced
2 medium carrots, finely diced
2 sticks celery, finely diced
2 medium red onions, diced
1 thumb-size piece of fresh ginger, peeled and finely diced

1 tsp cumin seeds
1 tbsp ground cumin
1½ litres vegetable stock
1 bunch fresh coriander, finely chopped
1 lemon (chopped zest and juice)
Salt and freshly ground black pepper
Coriander leaves for garnish

Heat olive oil in a large saucepan on medium heat. Add kumara, carrots, celery, onions, ginger, cumin seeds and ground cumin. Cook until onion is transparent. Add vegetable stock and bring to boil. Reduce heat and simmer until kumara is completely cooked. Remove from heat and allow soup to cool for 30 minutes. Using a blender or food processor, blend until smooth. Pour soup back into saucepan, return to boil then reduce heat. Mix in coriander, lemon zest and juice. Season with salt and pepper. This dish looks lovely garnished with coriander leaves.

FOOD FOR THOUGHT
Contrary to popular belief, ginger is not a root; it is a rhizome (underground stem). Two or three slices of ginger taken in one cup of hot water will settle indigestion and help stomach cramps. Place 10ml ginger syrup (available from health-food shops) in one cup of hot water at the onset of a cold, chill or flu. This is a wonderful way to warm, soothe and calm the body, and boost the immune system.

HEALTH BENEFITS
Ginger warms the insides; it stimulates circulation and brings warmth to cold extremities and to lungs and chest. It relieves nausea and is said to have anti-inflammatory properties that may help relieve painful joints. Research has shown that ginger has an antioxidant effect that slows down the ageing process. Avoid ginger if you suffer from ulcers or cannot tolerate heat.

coconut pumpkin dhal soup

Many years ago my Indian friend Rosa taught me the importance of spice and flavour when it comes to Indian cooking. This luscious, full soup has depth and texture; the coconut cream is decadent but also delicious. A good soup for a cold winter's day.

SERVES 8

4 tbsp olive oil
½ medium pumpkin, cubed 4cm
2 medium onions, diced
3 sticks celery, diced
2 medium carrots, diced
2 medium parsnips, diced
2 cups yellow lentils, rinsed
1 tbsp ground coriander
4 cloves garlic, peeled and crushed
1 thumb-size piece of fresh ginger, peeled and finely diced

2 fresh chillies, finely sliced
1 tsp brown mustard seeds
1 tsp yellow mustard seeds
1 tsp coriander seeds
1½ litres vegetable stock
2 cups coconut cream
1½ cups finely sliced fresh mint
Salt and freshly ground black pepper
Mint leaves for garnish

Heat olive oil in a large saucepan on medium heat. Add pumpkin, onions, celery, carrots, parsnips, lentils, ground coriander, garlic, ginger, chillies and seeds. Stir ingredients continuously and cook until onion is transparent. Add vegetable stock, bring to boil and reduce to simmer. Stir continuously and simmer for 30 minutes. Mix in coconut cream and mint. Return to boil. Season with salt and pepper. Serve hot, garnished with mint leaves. The success of this soup relies upon the continuous stirring of ingredients during boiling and simmering.

FOOD FOR THOUGHT

Celery can be stored in a plastic bag in the refrigerator for up to one week. It can also be blanched and frozen in plastic bags and used in recipes that call for cooked celery. Celery leaves can be chopped finely and used as a seasoning in soups and casseroles.

HEALTH BENEFITS

Celery was grown and used as a medicinal herb long before it was known for its culinary uses. It is often described as the guilt-free snack. Consisting of about 90 percent water, it hydrates the body and skin from within. Celery also contains potassium, folate and fibre. The greener variety of celery contains more vitamin C and folate.

roasted bell pepper and tomato soup with basil

Italians are famed for their skill with tomatoes, evident in this classic dish. The combination of tomatoes, roasted bell peppers and fresh nutmeg will charm your taste buds all the way to the bottom of the bowl!

SERVES 8

2 large red peppers
4 tbsp olive oil
2 medium red onions, diced
2 sticks celery, diced
2 medium carrots, diced
4 cloves garlic, peeled and crushed
1 tsp paprika

4 x 400g tins peeled plum tomatoes and juice
1 litre vegetable stock
¼ cup finely chopped fresh basil
1 whole nutmeg, finely grated
Salt and freshly ground black pepper
Chopped basil leaves for garnish

Pre-heat oven to 175°C. Place peppers in an oven dish and roast for approximately 30 minutes or until skins begin to blacken. Remove from oven and place in a sealed paper or plastic bag (this helps skins to fall away). Peppers should be allowed to cool slowly, inside bag, for at least 25 minutes. Remove from bag, peel, de-seed and dice finely. Set aside.

While peppers are cooling, heat olive oil in a large saucepan on medium heat. Add onions, celery, carrots, garlic and paprika. Cook until onion is transparent. Empty tomatoes and juice into a large bowl and, using your hands, mash or break up into small pieces. Add to ingredients in saucepan, bring to boil and reduce to simmer. Cook for 30 minutes, stirring continuously. Add vegetable stock and red pepper, return to boil, then reduce heat and simmer. Finally, add basil and nutmeg. Add salt and pepper to taste. Garnish with basil leaves. Serve with crusty fresh bread. Delicious!

FOOD FOR THOUGHT

Christopher Columbus discovered much more than America; he introduced the humble capsicum to Europe. Capsicums are known as bell peppers, sweet peppers, chillies, pimentos and so on. Red, yellow, orange, purple and green, the capsicum is the fruit of the plant, prepared as a vegetable.

HEALTH BENEFITS

Capsicums are packed with antioxidants (which fight free radicals and prevent premature ageing) and bioflavonoids (which help process vitamin C and maintain capillaries). Capsicums contain phytochemicals that help the body defend itself against cancer. Delicious cooked or raw, they also help to stimulate the stomach's protective mucous membranes.

chilled pear peppermint soup with vanilla

Edward Bunyard once said that a pear is a fruit that must be approached with discretion and reverence. With that in mind, gather your friends around the dinner table and allow their taste buds to do the talking.

SERVES 8

2 litres water
2 bay leaves
1 vanilla bean
1 carrot, finely sliced
4 tbsp honey
1 chilli, cut lengthways (optional)

8 large pears, cored, peeled and sliced
  (Beurre Bosc or Packham's Triumph)
1 lemon (chopped zest and juice)
¼ cup finely chopped peppermint leaves
  (or plain mint leaves)
Peppermint or mint leaves for garnish

First, make stock. Pour water into a large saucepan. Add bay leaves, vanilla bean, carrot, 2 tablespoons honey and chilli. Bring to boil, reduce heat and simmer for 30 minutes. Using a colander, strain stock. Retain liquid and vanilla bean only. Set aside.

Place sliced pears in a medium saucepan and add just enough water to cover pears. Add the remaining honey, cover and cook on medium heat for 15 minutes. Remove from heat, set aside. Split vanilla bean lengthways and scrape tar from the inside. Put vanilla tar, pears and juice from saucepan into blender or food processor. Purée until smooth. Mix into the stock. Add lemon zest, juice and peppermint leaves. Pour into a large bowl and refrigerate for 1 hour. To serve, place 3 or 4 ice cubes in chilled soup bowls, cover with soup and garnish with peppermint leaves.

FOOD FOR THOUGHT

Honey, often referred to as nature's sweetener, makes a lovely cleansing lotion. Take ¼ cup runny honey, 2 teaspoons whole milk and ½ teaspoon rosewater and mix until you have a smooth paste. Apply to skin as you would any other cleansing lotion. A couple of teaspoons of honey mixed with hot water or milk and drunk at bedtime will bring relief to those who are unable to sleep.

HEALTH BENEFITS

For years bacteriologists tested honey because they doubted that it could help destroy bacteria. They were proven wrong. The use of honey for its medicinal properties is recorded as far back as cave-dwelling days. Folk medicine records it as a cough remedy and a treatment for skin burns. It is non-irritating to the digestive tract, kind to the kidneys, alleviates hay-fever symptoms and helps to relieve gastric irritation.

courgette and thyme soup with asparagus

A classic soup using humble ingredients: potatoes, courgettes and garlic, topped off with asparagus spears and lemon. Simply divine.

SERVES 8

24 asparagus spears
6 tbsp olive oil
Cracked black pepper
3 medium potatoes, peeled and very
  finely diced
1 large onion, finely diced
1 large carrot, finely diced
2 sticks celery, finely diced

4 cloves garlic, peeled and crushed
8 medium courgettes, grated
1½ litres vegetable stock
¼ cup finely chopped fresh thyme
  (or lemon thyme)
1 lemon (chopped zest and juice)
Salt and freshly ground black pepper

Preheat oven to 100°C. Snap off the tough bottom part of the asparagus spears (usually white). Cut spears into 2cm lengths. Place a large, heavy-based frying pan on medium heat and add 2 tablespoons olive oil. Once oil is hot, add asparagus spears and cook for 3–4 minutes. Add a generous amount of cracked black pepper. Remove from pan, place in ovenproof dish, and keep warm in oven.

In a large saucepan, heat the remaining olive oil. Add potatoes, onion, carrot, celery and garlic. Cook until onion is transparent. Add courgettes and vegetable stock. Mix ingredients thoroughly. Remove from stove, pour into blender or food processor. Purée until smooth. Return mixture to saucepan and bring to boil. Reduce to simmer on low heat for 5 minutes. Add thyme, lemon zest and juice and season with salt and pepper. Ladle into soup bowls and decorate with asparagus spears.

FOOD FOR THOUGHT

Thyme creeps along through the ages. It is ideal for long, slow-cooked stews and soup dishes. In medieval times this herb was associated with courage and vigour. Ladies of the period would embroider sprigs of thyme onto gifts and clothing. Valiant knights bathed in thyme, presumably because they hoped it would sustain their courage!

HEALTH BENEFITS

The famous herbalist Nicholas Culpepper documented that thyme tea and infusions helped ease whooping cough, breathlessness and stomach cramps. Culinary thyme aids the digestion of fatty foods. Two teaspoons of thyme leaves in 1 cup of boiling water, twice a day, are said to soothe stomach upsets (allow to infuse for at least 8 minutes). Thyme leaves help strengthen the immune system. Thyme oil also has antiseptic properties.

pea, potato and brewer's yeast soup

This is a robust, full-flavoured soup of potatoes, leeks and onions combined with distinctive seasonings: wholegrain mustard and brewer's yeast. Give it a go — you will be pleasantly surprised.

SERVES 8

4 tbsp olive oil
4 or 5 medium Agria potatoes (or a similar floury potato), finely diced
2 medium leeks, finely diced
2 medium carrots, finely diced
2 medium onions, finely diced
2 medium courgettes, finely diced
4 cloves garlic, peeled and crushed
2 tsp wholegrain mustard

1 cup dry white wine
300g frozen peas
1½ litres vegetable stock
¼ cup finely chopped fresh dill
Salt and freshly ground black pepper
½ cup brewer's yeast
Brewer's yeast, Parmesan cheese and dill leaves for garnish

Place a large saucepan on medium heat. Add olive oil, potatoes, leeks, carrots, onions, courgettes, garlic and mustard. Cook for 7 minutes, stirring continuously. Add wine and 200g frozen peas. Cook for a further 5 minutes. Add 1 litre vegetable stock and bring to boil. Remove from heat and cool for 30 minutes. Pour into blender or food processor. Purée until smooth and return to saucepan. If soup is too thick, slowly add the remaining vegetable stock. Bring soup mixture back to boil, add the remaining peas, reduce heat and simmer for 2 minutes. Add dill and season generously with salt and pepper.

Place a frying pan on medium heat, add brewer's yeast and toast until brown and crispy (approximately 1 minute). To serve, ladle soup into bowls and sprinkle with toasted brewer's yeast and Parmesan. Garnish with dill leaves.

FOOD FOR THOUGHT

Before you pop the brewer's yeast back into the cupboard, mix 2½ tablespoons with 2 tablespoons avocado oil until you have a smooth brown paste. Using your hands, apply mask to face, let it dry, rinse off with warm water and moisturise as usual. Your skin will feel wonderful.

HEALTH BENEFITS

Brewer's yeast contains more than 15 amino acids and loads of vitamins and minerals. It helps maintain healthy skin, hair, eyes, digestive tract and liver. The amino acids found in brewer's yeast are often referred to as the building blocks of life and as such are vital also for healthy muscle tissue, organs, cells and hormones.

spinach and parsley soup

Some people do not like the look of green soups. Trust me: this green soup is delicious and truly divine when freshly made.

SERVES 8

1½ litres vegetable stock
4 tbsp olive oil
2 medium red onions, diced
2 medium carrots, diced
2 sticks celery, diced
1 parsnip, diced

4 cloves garlic, peeled and crushed
2 medium courgettes, diced
500g spinach, finely sliced
150g parsley, finely chopped
Salt and freshly ground black pepper
Parsley sprigs for garnish

Heat 1 litre vegetable stock. Meanwhile, place a large saucepan on medium heat. Add olive oil, onions, carrots, celery, parsnip and garlic. Cook until onion is transparent (approximately 4–5 minutes). Add courgettes, cook for a further 4 minutes. Add the hot stock. Bring to boil and remove from heat. Cool for 1 hour. Once soup is cooled, pour into blender or food processor and blend, slowly adding spinach and parsley. Add the remaining vegetable stock to blender and purée until soup is smooth and thick. Return soup to saucepan, bring to boil and season with salt and pepper. Serve hot, garnished with parsley sprigs.

FOOD FOR THOUGHT

Parsley — the perfect dressing for soups, fish, scrambled eggs and other dishes — is often pushed to the side of the plate, taken back to the kitchen and thrown out. However, both main types — curly parsley (traditional) and flat-leaf (Italian) — are rich in minerals and vitamins. The stalks, which seldom even get onto your plate, contain more flavour and vitamins than the leaves. Chewing parsley freshens the mouth and prevents onion and garlic breath.

HEALTH BENEFITS

Parsley is unique in that it contains more vitamin C than any other food. Vitamin C is a powerful antioxidant. Parsley contains carotene, potassium, folate, iron and calcium. It also helps the body eliminate excess fluid. Eat parsley to nourish your skin and body.

noodles, pasta & rice

sendai soba noodles with avocado

kata coconut noodles

cashew basmati rice

bergamo peasant spaghetti

roasted pumpkin and pine nut pasta

wild rice risotto

sendai soba noodles with avocado

Visits to Japan while working on rock 'n' roll tours introduced me to Japanese cuisine and principles of health. This dish combines noodles, kumara, broccoli and avocado. Add a pristine sweep of plum vinegar and sesame oil and you have a dish that will rock any palate.

SERVES 4

DRESSING
2 tbsp roasted sesame oil
2 tbsp umeboshi or brown rice vinegar
2 tbsp tamari or light soy sauce
4 tbsp water

VEGETABLES AND NOODLES
1 large kumara or sweet potato, cooked, peeled and cut into small cubes
1 small head of broccoli, cut into small flowerets and blanched

1 medium carrot, cut into matchsticks
¼ cucumber, cut into matchsticks
5 spring onions, finely sliced
2 tbsp roasted sesame seeds
200–250g dried soba (buckwheat) noodles, cooked (see below) and cooled
1 tbsp roasted sesame oil
2 firm avocados, peeled and cut into small cubes
Slices of pickled ginger for garnish

You can make the dressing for this dish the day before. Simply place the oil, vinegar, tamari and water into a jar, screw the lid on and shake until all ingredients are combined thoroughly. Pop into fridge until ready to use.

To make the noodle dish, combine the kumara, broccoli, carrot, cucumber, spring onions and sesame seeds in a large bowl and toss. Add noodles, avocados and most of the dressing and toss again. Serve into 4 noodle bowls and spoon remaining dressing over noodles. Garnish with a few slices of pickled ginger. Can be served hot or cold.

COOKING SOBA (BUCKWHEAT) NOODLES

Fill a large pot with 3 litres water and bring to boil. Drop noodles into boiling water, making sure they do not stick together. Add enough cold water to take them off the boil. Return to boil and once again, add enough cold water to take them off the boil. Taste noodles. If they are not al dente (firm to the centre), repeat the cold-water process. Once noodles are cooked, drain them, rinse with cold water for 20 seconds and drain again. Add 1 tablespoon roasted sesame oil and toss.

FOOD FOR THOUGHT

Avocados: I love them — though sadly one little avocado contains around 350 calories. Avocados do also contain antioxidants that help keep free radicals at bay. My motto is to eat half and slap the other half on your face! Skin and mash ½ ripe avocado, add 1 teaspoon freshly squeezed lemon juice and mix thoroughly until you have a smooth paste. Pat over face and neck and leave on for at least 15–20 minutes. Rinse, dry and moisturise as usual.

HEALTH BENEFITS

Avocados are in fact a fruit that yields an abundance of vitamins and minerals as well as heart-healthy mono-unsaturated fat. The vitamin E in avocados is a powerful antioxidant known to slow the ageing process and protect against heart disease and some forms of cancer. Avocados contain more potassium than bananas and also contain magnesium, which helps produce energy and is important for relaxation. The folate in avocados promotes healthy cell and tissue development. Research suggests that avocados help relieve morning sickness — worth a try!

kata coconut noodles

This dish is well worth the effort, with oodles of noodles. Udon noodles are a thick, cream-coloured wheat noodle, similar to spaghetti. Available in most supermarkets all year round, they are economical, easy to cook and provide a good source of carbohydrates. All the equipment you need to create a delicious, nutritious dish is a wok, a pot, a fork, a spoon and a noodle bowl.

SERVES 4

4 tbsp light olive oil
1 tsp cumin seeds
½ tsp yellow mustard seeds
½ tsp brown mustard seeds
1 tsp finely sliced lemongrass
1 large onion, sliced
1 medium carrot, cut into matchstick-size
  pieces
½ cauliflower, cut into small flowerets
1 tsp ginger paste
1 tsp garlic paste
1 tsp green curry paste

6 fresh curry leaves (optional)
2 fresh lime leaves (optional)
2 fresh medium to hot chillies (optional)
¼ green cabbage, cut into chunky squares
¼ red cabbage, cut into chunky squares
2 medium courgettes, sliced into rounds
2 cups coconut cream
1 tbsp brown sugar
1–2 cups vegetable stock
1 bunch fresh coriander, roughly chopped
250g fresh udon noodles
Salt

Fill a 4-litre pot with water, bring to boil, turn down heat and leave to simmer gently. Place a large wok on medium heat. Heat olive oil in wok, add cumin and mustard seeds, lemongrass, onion, carrot, cauliflower and ginger, garlic and curry pastes. Add curry and lime leaves and chillies, if desired. Cook for 5 minutes, tossing ingredients continually. Add green and red cabbage, courgettes, coconut cream, sugar, 1 cup vegetable stock and coriander. Cook for a further 3 minutes. Meanwhile, drop noodles into the boiling water. Boil for 2 minutes. Drain noodles and add to ingredients already simmering in wok. Season with salt. If sauce is too thick, add more stock. Noodles should be completely immersed in sauce. If using curry and lime leaves, remove them from dish before serving. Serve from a large noodle bowl.

FOOD FOR THOUGHT

Washing your face in cabbage water will result in a smoother, more youthful-looking skin.

HEALTH BENEFITS

Cabbage juice helps boost the immune system, brings relief to stomach ulcers, is good for acne and helps ward off colds, nasty coughs and flu. The greenest cabbage leaves contain most of the nutrients. Cabbage is a good source of iron; chlorophyll; vitamins A, B and C; and some minerals, including calcium and magnesium. For maximum nutritional value, eat cabbage raw. Eaten raw, lightly steamed or taken in the form of a juice, cabbage is an excellent remedy for those recuperating from illness or just feeling a little run-down.

cashew basmati rice

Your dinner guests will think you are a wizard when you serve up this simple, yet vibrant, wok-fried rice. Absolutely brilliant!

SERVES 4

4 cups basmati rice, cooked, cooled and
   refrigerated overnight
4 tbsp olive oil
1 large onion, diced
2 medium carrots, diced
2 sticks celery, diced
1 tsp yellow mustard seeds
1 tsp cumin seeds
½ tsp ground turmeric
1 tsp garlic paste

1 tsp ginger paste
3 medium courgettes, cut in half lengthways
   and sliced
1 tbsp green curry paste
½ cup roughly chopped fresh coriander
1 cup lightly roasted cashew nuts
200g spinach, finely sliced
Salt
½ cup lightly roasted desiccated coconut
   and juice of 1 lemon for garnish

Prepare rice as directed 1 day ahead. Place a large wok on medium heat and add olive oil, onion, carrots, celery, mustard and cumin seeds, turmeric, garlic and ginger pastes. Cook for 5 minutes. Add courgettes and curry paste. Cook for a further 3 minutes. Add cold rice to ingredients in wok and mix thoroughly. Cook for 3–4 minutes, continually turning rice. Add coriander, cashew nuts and spinach, and toss for at least 1 minute. Season with salt and garnish with coconut and lemon juice. Serve immediately.

FOOD FOR THOUGHT

In my grandmother's day, half an onion was left in the room of an invalid. The antiseptic vapour would cleanse the atmosphere. If you are suffering from a persistent sore throat or cough, slice a couple of large onions into thin rings, drizzle completely with honey, cover with cling film, and leave over- night. Strain off the juice and drink a small amount every two hours. It really is very pleasant.

HEALTH BENEFITS

Research shows that onions help fight infection and heart disease and that a diet high in vegetables, such as onions, may lower the risk of some cancers. Onion juice can relieve sore throats, colds, sinusitis, mucous and catarrh conditions.

bergamo peasant spaghetti

This is one of my favourite spaghetti dishes. Drinking grappa with Antonio Perna of Bergamo in Northern Italy, I learnt a lot about cooking great spaghetti. Ciao bella, Antonio.

SERVES 4

4 tbsp olive oil
2 red onions, finely sliced
3 medium courgettes, cut in half lengthways
   and sliced
6 cloves garlic, peeled and crushed
2 chillies, finely diced
½ cup white wine

300g dried spaghetti, cooked as below
½ cup finely chopped parsley
½–¾ cup breadcrumbs
½ cup finely grated Parmesan cheese
Salt
Finely grated Parmesan cheese for garnish

Place a large, heavy-based frying pan on medium heat. Add olive oil, onions, courgettes, garlic and chillies. Cook until onion is transparent. Add wine and cooked spaghetti (see below) and toss all ingredients in pan. In a bowl, combine parsley, breadcrumbs and Parmesan. Sprinkle dry ingredients through spaghetti mixture. Toss continually until spaghetti is coated with all the ingredients. Season with salt. To serve, place in a large, warm bowl and garnish with Parmesan.

HOW TO COOK SPAGHETTI

Fill a large pot with 3 litres of water, bring to boil and add the spaghetti, stirring for a few minutes to ensure strands do not stick together. Continue boiling, uncovered, until the pasta is al dente (just firm to the centre when you taste it). When spaghetti is cooked, drain and toss gently.

FOOD FOR THOUGHT

Peel a few garlic cloves, pop them in a jar, completely cover with honey, replace lid and sit jar in a warm place until the garlic cloves become translucent (about 5–6 hours). Strain and use the juice as a remedy for coughs and colds. One teaspoon every couple of hours is sufficient.

HEALTH BENEFITS

Crushed garlic releases allicin. Allicin is the key to garlic's health-giving properties because it has strong antibiotic qualities. Garlic performs a cleansing and disinfecting process as it passes through the body. It also causes the body to sweat and can help to reduce a fever.

roasted pumpkin and pine nut pasta

Served with a classic salad, this dish is a downright funky number with lots of surprising flavours. Pine nuts, basil, garlic and fennel bring tremendous life to an Italian-inspired pasta recipe.

SERVES 4

½ pumpkin (approx 1.5kg), peeled and
   cubed 1cm
Olive oil
1 tsp paprika
Cracked black pepper
300g dried farfalle (bow-tie) pasta
4 tbsp olive oil
2 red onions, sliced
4 cloves garlic, peeled and crushed

1 bulb of fennel, diced (save leaves for garnish)
¾ cup dry white wine
200g spinach, finely sliced
½ cup roughly chopped fresh basil
½ cup lightly roasted pine nuts
Salt and freshly ground black pepper
150g feta, cubed
Fennel leaves for garnish

Pre-heat oven to 175°C. Place pumpkin on a roasting tray, drizzle with a little olive oil, and sprinkle with paprika and cracked black pepper. Roast for 30 minutes or until the edge of the pumpkin begins to blacken. Remove from oven and set aside to cool. Cook pasta, drain and set aside.

Place a large, heavy-based frying pan on medium heat. Add the second measure of olive oil, onions, garlic and fennel. Cook for 4 minutes, tossing ingredients continually. Add wine and cook for a further 2 minutes, then add spinach, basil, pine nuts and pasta. Toss ingredients in pan, then add pumpkin. Season with salt and pepper. Add feta, toss again and serve garnished with fennel leaves.

FOOD FOR THOUGHT

Pine nuts make a versatile addition to many dishes, whether raw, roasted, ground, used in sauces or as a garnish on salads. They should be stored in tightly sealed containers in the fridge. Pine nuts also freeze well and will keep for up to 6 weeks in the freezer. To make a lovely facemask, blend ½ cup pine nuts with enough goat's milk to make a smooth paste. Apply to face and neck and leave on for 20 minutes. Rinse, pat dry and moisturise as usual.

HEALTH BENEFITS

Nutritionists are now advocating eating small quantities of nuts a couple of times a week to reduce the risk of heart disease and lower blood cholesterol. Nuts contain essential fats, vitamins and minerals — and peanuts, walnuts and cashews are also good sources of protein. If you have been leaving nuts out of your cooking, it's time to put them back in: they are fuel for the body.

wild rice risotto

On the American Indian calendar, the September moon is called the Wild Rice Moon. Wild rice was an important part of the Native American diet as it has a high protein content and can be stored easily. A risotto with a real difference, this dish really enhances the roasted, nutty flavour of the wild rice.

SERVES 4

250g wild rice
4 tbsp olive oil
1 red onion, sliced
2 medium red peppers, sliced
2 cups sliced button mushrooms
4 medium courgettes, sliced
1 tsp paprika
3 cloves garlic, peeled and crushed
¾ cup dry white wine
2 cups finely sliced spinach

¾ cup finely grated Parmesan cheese
Fresh mint leaves and grated Parmesan
  cheese for garnish

RISOTTO SAUCE
¼ pumpkin (approximately 900g),
  peeled, cooked and puréed
1 tsp ginger paste
1 tbsp finely chopped fresh mint
Salt

Pre-heat oven to 175°C. Fill a 2-litre pot with water. Add wild rice, bring to boil and reduce to simmer. Cook for approximately 25–30 minutes, until rice expands. Drain and set aside. Meanwhile, place a large, cast-iron frying pan on medium heat. Add olive oil, onion, peppers, mushrooms, courgettes, paprika and garlic. Cook until onion is transparent (approximately 4–5 minutes). Add wine and cook for a further 2 minutes. Add cooked rice, spinach and Parmesan. Mix all ingredients together thoroughly. Place frying pan in oven and bake for 10 minutes. While risotto is baking, make sauce.

Place a small frying pan on medium heat. Add pumpkin purée, ginger paste and mint. Bring to boil, simmer for 2 minutes and season with salt. Remove risotto from oven and cover with pumpkin sauce. Garnish with mint leaves and Parmesan.

FOOD FOR THOUGHT
Ancient Egyptians are said to have been the first to discover the medicinal qualities of the olive leaf. Greek legend favours the olive tree and refers to it as the tree of wisdom or the tree of life. Moisturise dry skin with olive oil. All you need is 4 tablespoons pure olive oil and 1 peeled, de-stoned avocado. Pop both in a blender and purée until smooth. Apply to face, leave for 15 minutes and then rinse off.

HEALTH BENEFITS
The leaf of the olive produces an extract known as oleuropine, considered to be a wonderful antioxidant and a natural antibiotic. Research now shows that olive oil contributes to a healthy heart and bones and also that it may help reduce levels of cholesterol, increase blood flow and bring relief to painful joints. Olive oil is easily digested and absorbed into the system. It can be used in salads and is a healthy substitute for butter.

vegetable salads

roasted red pepper, french bean and
  cos lettuce salad

balsamic beetroot

broccoli, cashew and marinated tofu salad

roasted parsnip, beetroot and couscous salad

watercress and marinated mushroom salad

chilled aubergine and coconut salad

peanut noodle salad

chilled orange, cucumber, walnut and
  yoghurt rice salad

roasted red pepper, french bean and cos lettuce salad

This recipe dates back to my days at The Melba in Courthouse Lane, Auckland. Increase the mustard and seasonings to make it even more robust, if that's your preference.

SERVES 4

4 large red peppers
4 tbsp olive oil
2 tbsp apple cider vinegar
2 cloves garlic, peeled and crushed
1 tsp wholegrain mustard
Salt and freshly ground black pepper
1kg small new potatoes, cooked, cooled and cut in half

200g French beans, blanched and cut into 2cm lengths
1 bunch parsley, finely chopped
1 red onion, finely diced
2 sticks celery, diced
16 kalamata olives
1 cos lettuce, cut into chunky squares
Parsley sprigs for garnish

Pre-heat oven to 175°C. Place peppers in an oven dish and roast for approximately 30 minutes or until skins begin to blacken. Remove from oven and place in a sealed paper or plastic bag (this helps skins to fall away). Peppers should be allowed to cool slowly, inside bag, for at least 25 minutes. Remove from bag, peel, de-seed and dice finely. Set aside.

To make dressing, place olive oil, vinegar, garlic, mustard, salt and pepper in a small jar. Screw lid on and shake thoroughly to combine ingredients.

In a large bowl, combine potatoes, beans, parsley, onion, celery, olives and peppers. Season with salt and pepper, add dressing and toss. To serve, place cos lettuce in a soup or pasta bowl and spoon salad ingredients on top. Garnish with parsley sprigs.

FOOD FOR THOUGHT
Sliced and chilled raw potato is an excellent booster for tired eyes. If you run out of your favourite exfoliating products, simply cut a potato in half and rub the exposed side over your skin. The starch from a grated potato soothes sunburn. Tired hands love mashed potato mixed with olive oil to form a soft paste — it gives them a new lease of life.

HEALTH BENEFITS
Potatoes contain a substantial amount of vitamin C and are a good source of fibre, carbohydrate and potassium. They are thought to contain antiviral and anti-inflammatory properties. Cooked in their jackets or skins, potatoes retain much of their nutritional value.

balsamic beetroot

Developed during summer holidays at Medlands Beach on Great Barrier Island and visits to Opononi in the Hokianga, this dish is now a favourite that I love to share with friends and students. The technique is definitely Italian.

SERVES 4

1 cup extra-virgin olive oil
3 large beetroot, scrubbed and finely
  sliced
250ml Italian balsamic vinegar

4 cloves garlic, peeled and crushed
1 tbsp fresh rosemary
Salt
Lettuce, finely chopped

Place a heavy-based frying pan on medium heat, add 2 tablespoons olive oil and lay enough rounds of beetroot side by side to cover base of pan. Do not stack or overlap. Pan-fry both sides of beetroot until edges are crisp (3–4 minutes each side). Be careful not to have the heat too high or leave the stove, because beetroot burns very easily. Remove from pan and drain on paper towels. Repeat with the rest of the beetroot and olive oil. Place beetroot in vinegar; add garlic and rosemary. Season with salt. Marinate for 1 hour. For best results, frequently stir beetroot through the marinade during this time. Serve over lettuce, to make an interesting salad.

FOOD FOR THOUGHT

Rosemary is for remembrance. Wear a sprig in your lapel and you won't forget a thing all day. Boil the leaves in water, strain and add to your bath, relax and enjoy. Folk medicine advocates drinking rosemary tea to treat arthritis. Worth a try!

HEALTH BENEFITS

Rosemary is an excellent tonic and the ideal herb to overcome exhaustion because it is uplifting and energising. Rosemary helps circulation, stimulates digestion and helps improve liver function. The essential oil of rosemary soothes aching limbs.

broccoli, cashew and marinated tofu salad

An Asian-style salad with a French nouvelle twist. Full of textures and striking tastes, it is refreshing to the palate and a great energy food. This is a dish that teaches you how to use tofu and enjoy it as well!

SERVES 4

1 large head of broccoli, cut into flowerets
1 block firm tofu
2 tbsp olive oil
½ cup tamari or light soy sauce
2 tbsp roasted sesame oil
1 thumb-size piece of ginger, finely grated
1 lemon (chopped zest and juice)
1 cup roasted cashew nuts

1 large carrot, grated
1 bunch coriander, roughly chopped
2 tbsp roasted sesame seeds
1 bunch spring onions, finely sliced
Salt and freshly ground black pepper
1 iceberg lettuce, cut into fine chiffonnade (very fine slices)
Coriander leaves for garnish

Blanch and refrigerate broccoli. Cut tofu into 3 equal slices and drain on a paper towel (approximately 2 minutes). Place a large, heavy-based frying pan on medium heat, add olive oil and pan-fry tofu until golden-brown on both sides. Remove and drain on a paper towel. Place tofu on a flat plate to cool and spoon 2 tablespoons tamari over it. Turn tofu continually to absorb as much of the tamari as possible. When cool, cut into 3cm cubes, return to the flat plate and make dressing.

To make dressing, place the remaining tamari, sesame oil, ginger and lemon zest and juice in a jar. Screw lid on and shake until ingredients are combined thoroughly. Set aside. In a large bowl, combine broccoli, tofu, cashew nuts, carrot, coriander, sesame seeds and spring onions. Season with salt and pepper, then toss. To serve, place lettuce on a plate and cover with tossed ingredients. Spoon dressing over salad. Garnish with coriander.

FOOD FOR THOUGHT

Tofu's porous texture readily absorbs the flavours of other ingredients, making it perfect for both savoury and sweet dishes. Firm tofu works well in salads and stir-fries. Silken tofu is perfect for purée or mash. You can make a face-pack with 3 tablespoons each of silken tofu and rice flour. Mash the tofu and mix into the flour until you have a soft paste. Apply to face and allow to dry. Remove with lukewarm water. Tofu masks are soothing on the skin and have often been used to treat acne.

HEALTH BENEFITS

Tofu is a versatile meat alternative. It is an excellent source of protein, calcium, iron, magnesium and selenium. Both natural and conventional practitioners recommend that menopausal women eat tofu, and take soymilk and other soy-based products, to ease hot flushes and other symptoms.

roasted parsnip, beetroot and couscous salad

The familiar comfort of roasted vegetables, served on a bed of couscous and decorated with olives . . . Freshly made and seasoned correctly, this dish is simply divine.

SERVES 4

4 medium parsnips, cut into 3cm x 2cm strips
2 medium beetroot, cut as above
3 medium carrots, cut as above
3 medium red onions, quartered
16 kalamata olives
1 bulb of garlic, separated into cloves,
   with skin on

2 tsp chopped fresh rosemary
Salt and freshly ground black pepper
4 tbsp olive oil
2 cups couscous
Boiling water
2 lemons (finely chopped zest and juice)
Sprig of fresh rosemary for garnish

Pre-heat oven to 175°C. In a large roasting tray, place parsnips, beetroot, carrots, onions, olives, garlic and rosemary. Add salt and pepper, drizzle olive oil over ingredients and mix thoroughly. Cook for 40–45 minutes, remove from oven and set aside.

Place couscous in a large bowl and pour in just enough boiling water to cover. Season with salt and pepper, whisk with a balloon whisk, cover and set aside for 10 minutes until water is totally absorbed. Add lemon zest. To serve, spoon couscous onto a flat plate, top with roasted vegetables and drizzle lemon juice over salad. Garnish with rosemary.

FOOD FOR THOUGHT
Beetroot is very low in calories. The Romans used it to fight fever. A juice made from carrots, beetroot and parsley is an excellent remedy for stomach cramps.

HEALTH BENEFITS
Beetroot is rich in iron, potassium, folic acid, phosphorous and many other vitamins and minerals. It stimulates production of red blood cells and is an excellent blood and liver cleanser.

watercress and marinated mushroom salad

I love the peppery, almost mustard bite of strong watercress. Combine that with sweet kumara and marinated mushrooms and you have a lush green salad. This is a favourite Musical Knives recipe with a distinct New Zealand influence.

SERVES 4

2 large kumara or sweet potatoes, cubed 1cm
3 red onions, quartered
8 tbsp olive oil
Salt and freshly ground black pepper
3 cups button mushrooms
1 cup dry white wine
½ cup finely chopped parsley
2 tbsp Dijon mustard

2 tbsp balsamic vinegar
1 tbsp runny honey
2 cloves garlic, peeled and crushed
1 large bunch of watercress, roughly chopped
1 cup lightly roasted pine nuts
½ cup lightly roasted sesame seeds
Sesame seeds for garnish

Pre-heat oven to 175°C. In a roasting tray, toss kumara and onions in 2 tablespoons olive oil. Season with salt and pepper. Roast for 35 minutes or until kumara becomes crispy. Remove from oven and set aside.

Place a large, heavy-based frying pan on medium heat. Add another 2 tablespoons olive oil and mushrooms. Cook until mushrooms begin to brown. Add wine, parsley and mustard. Cover pan, reduce heat to simmer and cook for 10 minutes. Remove from heat. Set aside to cool and marinate.

To make dressing, place the remaining olive oil, vinegar, honey, garlic and salt and pepper in a jar. Screw lid on and shake until ingredients are combined thoroughly.

In a large bowl, place kumara, onions and mushrooms. Add watercress, pine nuts and sesame seeds, and toss well. To serve, arrange in shallow salad bowls, spoon over dressing and garnish with sesame seeds.

FOOD FOR THOUGHT

If you think about it, there can hardly be a household in the world that does not have some kind of mustard in its kitchen cupboards. Mustard and balsamic vinegar make a nice simple dressing. Mix 4 tablespoons balsamic vinegar and 2 tablespoons mustard, add honey to taste and the result is delicious.

HEALTH BENEFITS

Mustard has antiseptic, digestive and stimulating properties. Mustard increases saliva, which in turn stimulates the appetite. In some cases, too much mustard can irritate the stomach but in moderate amounts it is said to neutralise toxins and help ward off stomach upsets. Mustard powder is also used to relieve congestion and clear the sinuses.

chilled aubergine and coconut salad

I love the texture of the chilled aubergine in this lightly spiced salad. Serve with a crispy French loaf and you have an excellent picnic on a hot summer's day.

SERVES 4

2 large aubergines
1 tbsp sea salt
1 tbsp ground cumin
1 tsp turmeric
200ml olive oil
400ml coconut cream
2 onions, finely diced
1 red pepper, finely diced

2 courgettes, finely diced
2 sticks celery, finely diced
1 thumb-size piece of ginger, grated
1 bunch coriander leaves, roughly chopped
Salt and freshly ground black pepper
2 cups blanched and finely sliced spinach
Coriander leaves for garnish

To prepare the aubergines, cube 1cm, then toss immediately in sea salt. Allow to stand for 10 minutes, rinse in cold water and drain on paper towels.

Place aubergine in a large bowl and toss with cumin and turmeric. Place a large, heavy-based frying pan on medium heat and cover base with olive oil. Add aubergine and cook until soft to the centre (3–4 minutes). Set aside.

Place coconut cream, onions, red pepper, courgettes, celery, ginger, coriander and aubergine in a large bowl. Season well with salt and pepper. Make sure ingredients are combined thoroughly and chill for 30 minutes. To serve, place a small bed of spinach on a flat plate, spoon salad on top and garnish with coriander leaves.

FOOD FOR THOUGHT

Salting before cooking will draw moisture from the aubergine, which reduces the amount of oil soaked up during the frying process. Aubergines will keep in the fridge for about 5 days but they are best used when fresh.

HEALTH BENEFITS

Aubergines are a member of the infamous nightshade family of plants, to which some people are sensitive. They do contain some protein, fat and fibre, and research scientists in the USA have recently stated that aubergines contain high levels of one of the most powerful antioxidants produced in plant tissues.

peanut noodle salad

Fast food at its best. This dish is simple and substantial with strong, clear seasonings. Great served with extra chilli and a beer on the side.

SERVES 4

4 packets 2-minute noodles
6 tbsp sunflower oil
2 tbsp kécap manis sauce
2 tbsp tamari or light soy sauce
1 lemon (finely chopped zest and juice)
2 cloves garlic, peeled and crushed
2 chillies, finely chopped
Salt and freshly ground black pepper
1 cup unsalted, skinned and roasted peanuts

2 carrots, grated
2 red onions, diced
1 bunch spring onions, sliced
1 bunch coriander, roughly chopped
2 cups blanched and finely sliced spinach
1 iceberg lettuce, cut into fine chiffonnade
   (very finely sliced)
Coriander leaves for garnish

Cook noodles, toss in 2 tablespoons oil and set aside. To make dressing, place the remaining oil, manis and tamari sauces, lemon zest and juice, garlic, chillies, salt and pepper in a jar. Screw lid on and shake until ingredients are combined thoroughly.

Place noodles, peanuts, carrots, onions, spring onions, coriander and spinach in a large bowl. Pour dressing over the top and toss until all ingredients are combined. To serve, place a bed of lettuce on a plate and arrange noodle salad on top. Garnish with coriander.

FOOD FOR THOUGHT

Don't cut away the goodness; the best way to prepare carrots is to scrub them and cook them in as little water as possible. As with potatoes, baking or steaming carrots helps seal in their flavour. Carrots also make a good face mask. Use a couple of carrots (pulp or purée them in a blender), apply cooled pulp to face and neck. Leave on for at least 20 minutes, rinse and pat dry. A 'two for one' deal that will bring a glow to most skin types.

HEALTH BENEFITS

Carrots contain antioxidants and nutrients including beta-carotene, vitamins B and C, calcium and more. Beta-carotene is converted by the body into vitamin A, which is important for healthy cell growth and strengthening of the immune system. Carrots are low in fat and calories and yield carbohydrates, protein and fibre.

chilled orange, cucumber, walnut and yoghurt rice salad

A simple salad developed from a nouvelle cuisine-style recipe. The combination of cucumber, orange and walnut with mint and yoghurt can easily be prepared in advance and served with barbecue food.

SERVES 4

4 large oranges, segmented
1 medium telegraph cucumber, finely sliced
1 head of broccoli, cut into small flowerets
   and blanched
1 cup lightly roasted walnut pieces

½ cup roughly chopped fresh mint leaves
400ml natural yoghurt
Salt and freshly ground black pepper
500g jasmine rice
Fresh mint leaves for garnish

In a large bowl, combine oranges, cucumber, broccoli, walnuts, mint and yoghurt. Season generously with salt and pepper. Chill for 1 hour. Meanwhile, cook rice and cool. To serve, place a bed of rice on a flat plate, spoon salad on top and garnish with mint leaves.

FOOD FOR THOUGHT

Oranges make a lovely citrus hand-cream. All you need is 100ml melted cocoa butter, 100ml olive oil, 50ml orange juice and 3 drops orange essential oil. Melt cocoa butter, add olive oil and orange juice, and whisk until emulsified. Cool for 45 minutes. Place all ingredients except essential oil in a blender and blend for about 60 seconds. Decant into a bowl and add essential oil. Leave to settle for about 1 hour, whisk well and pour into a container ready for use. The cream will keep for about 4 days in the fridge.

HEALTH BENEFITS

Oranges contain vitamin C, which helps to build the body's defence system. They also contain pectin, a kind of soluble fibre that is thought to help reduce LDL cholesterol, regarded as the 'bad' type of cholesterol. Eating the whole fruit is best.

flans, frittata & roulade

peach and parmesan flan

spinach and cottage cheese flan

spinach, olive and asparagus
   filo parcels

green bean frittata

aubergine and ricotta roulade

florentine and goat cheese tart

peach and parmesan flan

This dish is slightly more savoury than sweet and I like serving it for lunch with chilled dry sherry. It reminds me of my visits to Spain.

SERVES 8

PASTRY
300g plain flour
1 tbsp castor sugar
¼ tsp salt
200g unsalted butter, cubed and softened
2 tbsp water

FILLING
500g castor sugar
60ml water
6 peaches, de-stoned and quartered
250g unsalted butter
100g Parmesan cheese, finely grated
200g breadcrumbs
3 eggs, whisked for 20 seconds

To make the pastry, mix flour, sugar and salt and rub butter in until the consistency is fine and crumbly. Mix water in; form into dough. Wrap in cling film and refrigerate for 1 hour. Roll pastry out on a cold floured surface and lay in a 30cm crinkled flan tin.

Pre-heat oven to 180°C. To make the filling, place 300g castor sugar and the water in a saucepan that is wide enough to lay peaches side by side in one layer. Add the peaches and bring to the boil. To prevent peaches sticking, gently move them around in pan as sugar dissolves. Once sugar has dissolved, reduce to simmer until you have a light, caramelised syrup. Remove from heat and cool for 5 minutes. Set aside. Melt butter, add remaining sugar and beat well. Mix in Parmesan, breadcrumbs and eggs. Fill two-thirds of pastry shell with butter mixture. Arrange peach quarters on top, gently pressing them down into butter mixture. Pour syrup from peach mixture over top of flan. Bake for 40 minutes or until pastry is golden-brown. Remove from oven and cool for 1 hour. This dish may be served as a dessert or as a savoury entrée with a light salad.

FOOD FOR THOUGHT

The nicest-tasting peaches smell sweet, yield to pressure and are free of blemishes and bruises. To ripen peaches, simply pop them into a paper bag with an apple, make some holes in the bag and leave for a couple of days. The apple helps to speed up the ripening process. Avoid peaches that have a green hue or are very hard: more often than not they do not ripen well.

HEALTH BENEFITS

Peaches contain vitamin C. In particular, dried peaches provide a good source of potassium, iron and niacin, which belongs to the B complex family of vitamins.

spinach and cottage cheese flan

Fresh nutmeg and lemon zest add a distinctive seasoning to this family favourite.

SERVES 4

Olive oil
1 x 500g packet puff pastry, thawed
500g spinach, blanched and finely sliced
Salt
1 whole nutmeg, finely grated

4 medium carrots, grated
Freshly ground black pepper
500g cottage cheese
1 lemon (chopped zest and juice)

Pre-heat oven to 180°C. Brush a 20cm x 20cm x 4cm baking dish with olive oil. Roll out two layers of pastry and place the first on base of dish. Season spinach with salt and nutmeg. Lay some of the spinach on top of the pastry base. Place a layer of carrot over spinach and season with salt and pepper. Season cottage cheese with lemon zest and juice and lay on top of carrots. Repeat layering process until baking dish is full. Compress layers and cover with pastry. Brush with olive oil, season with salt and pepper, and bake in oven for 20– 25 minutes until pastry is golden-brown. Slice and serve with salad and new potatoes.

FOOD FOR THOUGHT

Nutmeg and a couple of other ingredients make a lovely warming potpourri blend. You will need 2 whole nutmegs, 2 cinnamon sticks, ground ginger, 2 whole cloves, zest of 1 lemon and 1 lime. Grind the nutmeg; add it to the cinnamon and cloves. Add lemon and lime zest. Mix thoroughly. Add 2 drops of your favourite essential oils. Place in a zip-lock bag and allow essential oils to infuse other ingredients for 24 hours, then pop into a nice bowl. Particularly effective when placed near a warm fire on a cold winter's evening.

HEALTH BENEFITS

Nutmeg is excellent for indigestion and the stomach upsets associated with food poisoning. Nutmeg oil is used in massage to alleviate muscular pain. Its warming, stimulating properties are ideal for circulatory and joint ailments. Medieval medicine documents nutmeg as being helpful in strengthening mental activity.

spinach, olive and asparagus filo parcels

This dish can be prepared beforehand and thrown into the oven when guests arrive. While you make the parcels, cover the sheets of filo pastry with a damp tea-towel to prevent them drying out. I like serving these pastries with a fresh tomato and red onion salsa.

SERVES 4

Olive oil
1 x 500g packet filo pastry, thawed
500g spinach, blanched, finely sliced and dried
30 fresh asparagus spears (thin)

24 kalamata olives, de-stoned and roughly chopped
¾ cup finely grated Parmesan cheese
Salt and cracked black pepper

Pre-heat oven to 170°C. To make each parcel, lay 1 sheet of filo pastry on a clean, dry surface and brush lightly with olive oil. Fold all 4 edges of pastry over to make a narrow border. Lay a 20 cm-wide bed of spinach close to the pastry edge nearest you. Place 4 or 5 asparagus spears on the spinach bed. Sprinkle olives and Parmesan over spinach and asparagus. Season with salt and pepper. Fold outside edges of filo over filling, roll up and brush lightly with olive oil. Cook in oven for 25 minutes until golden-brown. Serve immediately.

FOOD FOR THOUGHT
Asparagus is considered to be a liver tonic and is said to help control breast tenderness and bloating during pre-menstrual tension. According to folklore, drinking the water of asparagus after it has been steamed is good for arthritis and urinary problems.

HEALTH BENEFITS
Spinach provides the body with a good supply of chlorophyll, which is kind to the liver and digestive tract and — believe it or not — is said to combat body odour.

green bean frittata

I love making frittatas. Filling the house with divine aromas while cooking, frittatas look gorgeous — puffy and golden-brown when served.

SERVES 8

5 eggs, lightly beaten
1 cup cream
½ cup finely grated Parmesan cheese
Salt and freshly ground black pepper
4 tbsp olive oil
4–5 medium potatoes, cooked and cubed 3cm

2 medium red onions, finely sliced
1 red pepper, de-seeded and finely sliced
200g French beans, cut into 4cm lengths
2 cloves garlic, peeled and crushed
½ cup finely chopped parsley

Pre-heat oven to 180°C. Place eggs, cream, Parmesan, salt and pepper in a bowl. Combine thoroughly and set aside. Place a deep, ovenproof frying pan on medium heat. Add olive oil, potatoes, onions, red pepper, beans and garlic. Cook until onion is transparent, continually tossing ingredients in pan. Add parsley and season well with salt and pepper. Pour in egg and cream mixture and place frying pan in oven to cook. Remove when top of frittata is golden-brown (approximately 40–45 minutes). Cool for 10 minutes, slice and serve with a roasted vegetable salad.

FOOD FOR THOUGHT

Eggs are great for softening and nourishing the skin. Egg white in particular is very soothing when applied to sore cracked skin. Smoothed over the face, it makes an excellent firming mask. If you drop an egg on the floor or workbench when you are cooking, don't panic. Cover the mess entirely with salt, leave it for 3–5 minutes and it will then be easy to clean up with paper towels.

HEALTH BENEFITS

Eggs are little powerhouses of nutrients. They are high in protein and they also have a high phosphorus content, which is good for strong bones and teeth. Egg whites are fat-free and the yolk of the egg contains vitamin D.

aubergine and ricotta roulade

One of my favourite Christmas recipes, this roulade must be made the night before. It is deliciously cool on a hot summer's day. The combination of oregano, capers and garlic is enhanced by the sweetness of the roasted red peppers, creating a stylish and substantial dish.

SERVES 8

2 red peppers
2 large aubergines
Salt
Olive oil
500g ricotta cheese

1 cup blanched and finely sliced spinach
1 tbsp finely chopped fresh oregano
1 tbsp finely chopped capers
4 cloves garlic, peeled and crushed
2 tbsp olive oil

Pre-heat oven to 180°C . Place peppers on a roasting tray and roast for approximately 30 minutes or until skins begin to blacken. Remove from oven and place in a sealed paper or plastic bag (this helps skins to fall away). Peppers should be allowed to cool slowly, inside bag, for at least 25 minutes. Remove from bag, peel, de-seed and dice finely. Set aside.

Cut aubergines lengthwise into 3cm slices. Lay slices on a flat tray and rub salt into surface. Leave for 30 minutes and then brush salt off. Liberally coat aubergine slices with olive oil. Place in oven and bake for 25 minutes. Remove from oven, set aside and allow to cool. In a large bowl, combine ricotta, peppers, spinach, oregano, capers, garlic and the 2 tablespoons olive oil.

Lay a piece of 30cm x 30cm cling film on a clean bench. Make a flat bed of aubergine by laying cooked slices horizontally across the film. Slices should slightly overlap each other. Spread ricotta mixture evenly across aubergine bed. Using cling film, roll up the mixture (like a swiss roll), ensuring cling film rolls around food, not into it. Twist ends of cling film tightly to seal. Once roll is tightly wrapped, place in fridge and leave overnight. Remove from fridge, peel off cling film and slice into rounds. Serve with a fresh green leafy salad.

FOOD FOR THOUGHT

Throw out the cooking fat; bring in the olive oil. The goodness in olive oil will keep your skin, heart and hair healthy.

HEALTH BENEFITS

Oregano is much more than a culinary herb. Research shows that it contains quercetin, said to inhibit some types of cancers. In folklore, oregano was used as an expectorant and a stomach tonic. Added to rich food, it may save you from those embarrassing intestinal gas moments.

florentine and goat cheese tart

This recipe reminds me of Paris and the stunning range of goat cheeses available there. A simple, elegant dish that can be made with a high-quality goat feta, it is most definitely at its best when soft goat cheese is used. This can be made as a large flan or small individual tartlets.

SERVES 8

PASTRY
150g unsalted butter, cubed and softened
2½ cups flour
½ tsp each salt and freshly ground black
  pepper
2 tbsp water

FILLING
3 large red onions, finely sliced
3 eggs, lightly beaten
50g butter, melted
½ cup finely chopped parsley
250g goat cheese, crumbled
2 cloves garlic, peeled and crushed
Salt and freshly ground black pepper

Pre-heat oven to 180°C . To make the pastry, mix butter into flour and add salt, pepper and water. Combine all ingredients by hand or use a food processor. Well-blended pastry should not crumble. If dough does crumble, add a little more water. Shape into ball, wrap in cling film and refrigerate for 30 minutes. Meanwhile, grease a 22cm flan dish and sprinkle with flour, then set aside. Remove pastry from fridge, roll out on a flat, dry surface and lay in flan dish. Make sure the sides of the pastry are firm and neat against flan dish. Bake in the oven for 15 minutes, remove and set aside to cool. (Do not prebake individual tartlets; simply fill pastry cases and bake for 20 minutes.).

Place onions in a roasting tray and roast for 20 minutes. Remove and cool. In a large bowl, combine eggs, butter, parsley, cheese, garlic, salt, pepper and onions. Mix thoroughly. Spoon into the pastry shell. Return to oven for 30 minutes, until top of mixture has browned slightly. Serve with a crispy green salad. Delicious!

FOOD FOR THOUGHT
Cayenne spices up culinary dishes and brings relief to aching teeth. Apply a few grains to the painful tooth; the pain will intensify at first but trust me, within a very short time the tooth should stop aching and carry you over until you visit your dentist.

HEALTH BENEFITS
Pepper is documented as one of the earliest known spices. It aids poor circulation, helps the immune system to combat viruses and infections and warms the body against chills. Cayenne, made from chillies, contains pain-relieving properties said to bring relief to arthritis sufferers.

legumes & grains

minty couscous with avocado
and orange segments

parsley, corn and tomato polenta served
with braised onions

lentilles vertes de puy
(french green lentil patties)

hazelnut fritters with yoghurt dressing

coconut chickpea curry with figs

black rice mushroom cakes

minty couscous with avocado and orange segments

Deceptively simple, this dish is a real star. It sparkles with bright orange segments, and the addition of mint makes it surprisingly refreshing.

SERVES 4

2 cups couscous
2 tbsp olive oil
Salt
3 oranges (segments and chopped zest)

2 avocados, diced
½ cup roughly chopped fresh mint leaves
Salt and freshly ground black pepper

Place couscous in a bowl. Add enough boiling water to cover completely. Add olive oil and salt. Mix thoroughly with a balloon whisk. Place a flat plate on top of bowl and let stand for 5 minutes. Fold in orange segments and zest, avocados and mint. Season with salt and pepper. Serve in a bowl on its own or on a bed of fresh garden salad. This recipe makes a fantastic accompaniment to seafood.

FOOD FOR THOUGHT

A couple of teaspoons of salt in a glass of warm water will soothe any sore throat. Mix a handful of ordinary salt or sea salt with 2 tablespoons vegetable oil and you have a simple but effective body scrub. Add 1 cup sea salt to your bath and soak in it for 15 minutes. It will help draw impurities from the skin.

HEALTH BENEFITS

Can't live with it; can't live without it. Every household has salt on the dining-room table because it is a basic commodity and the most commonly used seasoning. Too little can be as bad as too much. Excessive use of salt may upset other mineral levels within the body. A lack of salt in the diet may have an adverse effect on the liver and kidneys. Salt is essential but must be used in moderation.

parsley, corn and tomato polenta served with braised onions

Just as nice served hot or cold, this traditional savoury dish will satisfy many a hungry person.

SERVES 8

1 litre standard milk
500g butter
1½ cups polenta or semolina
3 eggs, lightly beaten
2 cups grated tasty cheddar cheese
1 whole nutmeg, finely grated
1¼ cups corn kernels
2 cups blanched and finely sliced spinach
½ cup chopped parsley

2 tomatoes, diced
Salt and freshly ground black pepper
¼ cup finely grated Parmesan cheese
½ cup roughly chopped almonds
2 tbsp olive oil
2 bay leaves
3 red onions, peeled and quartered
1 tbsp brown sugar
½ cup medium or dry white wine

Pre-heat oven to 180°C. Heat milk and butter in a saucepan until it boils. Reduce heat, add polenta or semolina and stir continuously to prevent lumps from forming: the mixture should have a smooth consistency. Quickly fold in eggs, cheddar, nutmeg, corn, spinach, parsley and tomatoes. Season with salt and pepper, then pour into a shallow casserole dish. Sprinkle with Parmesan and almonds. Cook in oven for 25 minutes or until golden-brown.

To make braised onions, place a heavy-based frying pan on medium heat. Add olive oil, bay leaves and onions and cook until onion is transparent. Add sugar and cook for 3–4 minutes. Add wine and cook for a further 3 minutes until wine has reduced. Spoon braised onions over cooked polenta slice and serve with steamed vegetables.

FOOD FOR THOUGHT
Tomatoes are excellent for oily skins, making them feel cleaner and tighter. Cut one tomato in half and rub on skin. Leave for 10 minutes and wash off with warm water. A paste of tomato juice and buttermilk will take the sting out of sunburn.

HEALTH BENEFITS
Tomatoes are bursting with lycopene, a powerful antioxidant that gives tomatoes their lovely rich red colour.

lentilles vertes de puy (french green lentil patties)

These lovely little French lentils are so adaptable. Surprisingly good with fish, they also bulk out a soup, casserole or ready-made salad instantly. The fennel in this recipe combines well with Dijon mustard. The patties can be served hot or cold.

MAKES 12 PATTIES

100ml olive oil
1 fennel bulb, finely diced
1 red onion, finely diced
2 sticks of celery, finely diced
¼ cup white wine
1 tbsp Dijon mustard
½ cup finely chopped parsley
200g Puy lentils (do not pre-soak)

4 medium potatoes, peeled and cubed 2cm
Salt and freshly ground black pepper
½ cup finely grated Parmesan cheese
½ cup flour
1 egg, whisked
1 cup breadcrumbs
1 lemon, cut into wedges, for garnish

Place a small saucepan on medium heat. Add 2 tablespoons olive oil, fennel, onion and celery. Cook until onion is transparent. Add wine and mustard, cook for a further 3 minutes, then add parsley. Turn mixture out into a bowl and set aside.

Cook lentils for 10 minutes, drain and set aside. Cook potatoes, then mash and season with salt and pepper. Mix lentils and Parmesan into mashed potato. Add fennel and onion mixture and combine thoroughly. Using your hands, compress and form the mixture into 12cm x 5cm patties. Take each patty and dust it with flour. Coat patties in whisked egg and roll them in breadcrumbs. Place a large, heavy-based frying pan on medium heat and cover bottom of pan with the remaining olive oil. Cook patties until golden-brown. Remove and drain on paper towels. Serve with lemon wedges and your favourite relish.

FOOD FOR THOUGHT

Lemon juice and olive oil make a lovely elbow softener. All you need is the juice of 1 lemon, 6 tablespoons olive oil and 1 tablespoon runny honey. Place ingredients in a sterilised jar, cover with lid and shake. Massage onto elbows daily. Watch that hard skin disappear.

HEALTH BENEFITS

Refreshing lemons are rich in potassium and vitamin C. Their many therapeutic qualities include natural antiseptic and purifying properties, and they can be used as a mild diuretic. A drink of lemon juice and warm water each morning helps clean the liver. Hot lemon drinks help fight infections, colds and flu.

hazelnut fritters with yoghurt dressing

Adapted from a spicy Indian recipe, these fritters are egg- and dairy-free thanks to the use of chickpea flour. To make a fantastic party food, reheat the fritters in the oven just before serving.

MAKES 12 TO 14 FRITTERS

250–275g chickpea or pea flour
75g lightly roasted hazelnuts, finely ground
150g spinach, finely sliced
1 tbsp brown mustard seeds
1 tbsp cumin seeds
2 tbsp ground coriander
2 tbsp baking powder
2 tbsp red curry paste

2 tbsp sea salt
100ml olive oil
Coriander leaves for garnish

DRESSING
2 cups natural yoghurt
¼ cup roughly chopped fresh coriander
¼ cup grated and salted telegraph cucumber

In a large bowl, place flour, hazelnuts, spinach, mustard and cumin seeds, ground coriander, baking powder, curry paste and salt. Add enough water to combine all the ingredients thoroughly into a porridge-like consistency. Leave for 5 minutes to allow ingredients to absorb water. If mixture is too thick, add more water.

Cover the base of a heavy frying pan with olive oil and place on medium heat. When oil is hot, spoon fritter mixture into pan. A good size for each fritter is 8–10cm wide. Cook until both sides are golden-brown. Remove and drain on paper towels. Set aside.

To make dressing, place yoghurt in a bowl. Add coriander and cucumber. Mix well and chill for 30 minutes. Garnish fritters with coriander leaves; serve with yoghurt dressing and a fresh salad.

FOOD FOR THOUGHT
Yoghurt is a fashionable and versatile food. It is good to eat and very effective as a home beauty aid. Natural yoghurt is kind to the skin and helps to remove surface impurities. Applied to the face on a regular basis it will leave the complexion fresh and smooth.

HEALTH BENEFITS
Yoghurt is high in protein and a valuable source of calcium; it also contains vitamins A, B and C and some minerals. Yoghurt is helpful in reducing the side-effects of antibiotics and yeast infections. Natural yoghurt containing live bifidus and acidophilus cultures promotes healthy intestines and is very good for the digestive and immune systems.

coconut chickpea curry with figs

A substantial meal, this dish is full of taste and texture and is very nutritious. The curry paste complements the sweetness of the figs, captured in a lush coconut cream.

SERVES 4

¼ small cabbage, finely sliced
½ cup chopped fresh coriander
6 tbsp olive oil
1 tbsp cumin seeds
1 large onion, diced
2 parsnips, diced
1 carrot, diced
4 cloves garlic, peeled and crushed
1 tbsp ground cumin

2 cups cooked chickpeas
1 tbsp green curry paste
8 dried figs, quartered
3 courgettes, sliced 1cm
250ml vegetable stock
1 cup coconut cream
Salt
½ cup lightly roasted coconut flakes
  for garnish

In a wok, fry cabbage and coriander in 2 tablespoons olive oil for 2 minutes. Set aside. Place a heavy-based saucepan on medium heat and add the remaining olive oil and the cumin seeds. Cook until seeds split or pop. Add onion, parsnips, carrot, garlic and ground cumin. Cook until onion is transparent. Add chickpeas, curry paste, figs, courgettes, vegetable stock and coconut cream. Bring to the boil and reduce to simmer. Cook for a further 10 minutes. Season with salt. Garnish with a sprinkle of coconut flakes and serve immediately with the cabbage and coriander on a bed of rice.

FOOD FOR THOUGHT

Did you know that ½ cup dried figs is said to provide the same amount of calcium as drinking ½ cup milk? Amazing.

HEALTH BENEFITS

Figs are fat- and cholesterol-free and are an excellent source of fibre, calcium and potassium. Dried figs make a calcium-rich snack and are a good energy food, especially when you are travelling.

black rice mushroom cakes

Thai black glutinous rice is fabulous in this recipe because of its sticky texture. These rice cakes make excellent travel snacks or picnic food.

MAKES 12 CAKES

2 cups uncooked Thai black glutinous rice
   (do not confuse with wild rice)
750ml water
1 stick cinnamon
2 cloves
4 tbsp olive oil
1 large onion, finely diced
2 large carrots, finely diced
1 thumb-size piece fresh ginger, peeled
   and finely diced

2 cloves garlic, peeled and crushed
100g button mushrooms, sliced
1 tbsp tamari or light soy sauce
½ cup finely sliced spring onions
1 cup arrowroot
Olive oil for frying
1 iceberg lettuce, finely sliced and left in a
   bowl of cold water with juice of 1 lemon
4 tbsp kécap manis sauce
Lemon wedges for garnish

Wash rice thoroughly. Fill a saucepan with the water, cinnamon, cloves and rice. Bring to the boil and reduce to simmer. Cook until rice is soft to the centre. Drain in a colander and discard cinnamon and cloves.

Place a large frying pan on medium heat. Add olive oil, onion, carrots, ginger, garlic and mushrooms. Cook for 10 minutes, stirring continuously. Reduce to simmer, mix in tamari and spring onions and then turn into a bowl to cool.

Combine black rice and mushroom mixture with 2 tablespoons arrowroot. Using your hands, make 12cm x 5cm rice cakes. Dust cakes with the remaining arrowroot. Return frying pan to medium heat and cover the base with olive oil. Add rice cakes and cook until golden-brown. Remove and drain on paper towels. Serve rice cakes on a bed of lettuce with manis sauce drizzled over them. Garnish with lemon wedges.

FOOD FOR THOUGHT

Arrowroot makes a lovely moisturising hand-mask. Warm 2 tablespoons glycerine and add 2 tablespoons arrowroot. Stir until mixture forms a paste. Add ½ teaspoon rosewater, 1000mg vitamin E capsule and 1 drop of your favourite essential oil. Stir well. Massage liberally over hands and arms until mask is absorbed into skin. Leave for 10 minutes. Rinse, dry and moisturise as usual. Your hands will feel silky and smooth.

HEALTH BENEFITS

Arrowroot has no flavour. It is used as a binder or thickener and is an easily digestible starch. It is soothing to stomachs and brings relief to bowel disorders.

seafood

smoked kahawai and leek salad

saucy salmon pilaf with coconut cauliflower

monkfish with almond dukkah
and scandinavian potatoes

celeriac fish soup with sage crostini

funky calamari on atami chinese greens

spiced terakihi fillets with
slow-roasted tomatoes

smoked kahawai and leek salad

I am sure you will agree that New Zealand smoked fish is in a class of its own. This dish is most definitely Pacific in its inspiration and application.

SERVES 4

400g new potatoes or small Jersey Bennes
4 medium leeks
8 tbsp olive oil
2 medium courgettes, sliced into rounds
2 cloves garlic, peeled and crushed
1 tbsp wholegrain mustard
2 tbsp ground walnuts

1 cup white wine
Salt and freshly ground black pepper
1 large smoked kahawai
½ cup chopped parsley
½ cup lightly roasted walnut halves
    for garnish

Place whole potatoes in a saucepan, cover with water and bring to the boil. Reduce to simmer and drain when just cooked. Cool and set aside.

Remove and discard the green parts of 3 leeks. Slice the green part of the fourth leek finely and set aside for garnish. Slice the white part of the leeks into 5cm rounds. Place 4 tablespoons olive oil in a large, heavy-based frying pan on medium heat, add white leeks and cook for 3 minutes. Add courgettes, garlic and mustard. Cook for 2 minutes, then add walnuts and wine. Cook for a further 2 minutes, remove from heat and set aside. Cut potatoes in half, place in a large bowl and season with salt and pepper. Add leek mixture, combine and set aside.

Using your hands, gently remove skin and bones from kahawai. Break fish into small flakes and sprinkle into potato and leek mixture. Add parsley and combine thoroughly. Set aside for 20 minutes. To make leek garnish, place the remaining olive oil in a heavy-based frying pan on medium heat. Add sliced green leek and cook until blackened and crispy. Drain on paper towels. Serve salad onto plates and garnish with crispy leek and walnut halves.

FOOD FOR THOUGHT
Use leeks to cure a persistent cough. Wash 1 leek, fold it in half lengthways and place in a muslin square. In a saucepan, cover the leek with water and cook until soft. Remove and cool. Squeeze juice from leek (through muslin cloth) into a glass. You could add honey to sweeten this remedy, but it works best when taken neat.

HEALTH BENEFITS
Leeks are plentiful in iron, magnesium, potassium and calcium. They help relieve sore throats. Taken regularly, they can be a simple yet effective tonic for the whole body.

saucy salmon pilaf with coconut cauliflower

The combination of salmon with rosemary is especially enticing and reminds me of the Italian restaurants where I worked in London. This is a mouth-watering dish served hot or cold. For best results, use good-quality rice.

SERVES 4

8 tbsp olive oil
1 large red onion, diced
1 large carrot, diced
1 red pepper, diced
1 tbsp fresh rosemary
2 tbsp currants
2 cloves garlic, peeled and crushed
1 cup white wine
2 cups uncooked basmati rice

½ teaspoon turmeric
1½ litres fish or vegetable stock
500g salmon fillets, cut into 2cm slices
Salt and freshly ground black pepper
1 tsp caraway seeds
1 medium cauliflower, cut into 1cm slices
1½ cups coconut cream
½ cup sliced spring onions
1 lemon, cut into wedges, for garnish

Pre-heat oven to 170°C. Place a large, heavy-based frying pan on medium heat and add 4 tablespoons olive oil, onion, carrot and red pepper. Cook for 3 minutes. Add rosemary, currants, garlic and wine. Cook for a further 2 minutes. Then mix rice and turmeric in thoroughly, continually working rice off the bottom of the pan. Pour mixture into a large ovenproof bowl. Heat stock and pour over ingredients in bowl. Totally submerse salmon slices in stock mixture and season with salt and pepper. Seal with tinfoil and bake in oven for 25 minutes.

While the salmon pilaf is baking, place a large wok on medium heat. Add the remaining olive oil and caraway seeds and cook for 1 minute. Add cauliflower and toss continually for 4 minutes. Add coconut cream, reduce to simmer and add spring onions. Season with salt and pepper. Cook for a further 2 minutes. Serve the salmon pilaf with coconut cauliflower on the side. Garnish with lemon wedges.

FOOD FOR THOUGHT

In preparation for the traditional Indian wedding ceremony, turmeric is combined with lemon juice and rubbed all over the body as a gentle cleanser.

HEALTH BENEFITS

Turmeric is a spice that contains curcumin. Apart from giving turmeric its yellow colour, curcumin is anti-inflammatory, eases stomach discomfort, helps prevent blood clotting and improves digestion by increasing the flow of bile from the gallbladder. Turmeric has for many years been used in Chinese medicine to treat a diverse range of disorders.

monkfish with almond dukkah and scandinavian potatoes

The first bite of succulent juicy monkfish always reminds me of crayfish. When served, this fish should be moist and juicy. I use an almond dukkah in this dish but any variety of dukkah will suffice.

SERVES 4

8 medium roasting potatoes (not peeled)
60ml olive oil
Salt and freshly ground black pepper
600g monkfish, sliced into 100g fillets
50g almond dukkah
4 medium carrots, finely sliced into rounds

2 cloves garlic, peeled and crushed
500g spinach, roughly chopped
1 lemon (finely chopped zest and juice)
Sea salt
40g lightly roasted almond slices
1 lemon, cut into wedges, for garnish

Pre-heat oven to 180°C. Cut potatoes into 5mm slices, cutting only three-quarters through. Place in a baking tray and drizzle with 20ml olive oil. Season with salt and pepper and bake in oven for 1 hour. Baste every 10 minutes. Cook until golden-brown.

Place monkfish fillets on baking tray, season with salt and pepper, dust with almond dukkah and drizzle with 20ml olive oil. Bake for 20– 25 minutes. When cut, fillets should be moist to the centre.

Heat the remaining olive oil in a large wok on medium heat, add carrots and cook for 4 minutes, then add garlic and spinach. Cook for 2 minutes, continually tossing ingredients in wok. Add lemon zest and juice, sea salt and almond slices. Mix thoroughly and serve onto plates, with fish on spinach bed and potatoes alongside. Garnish with lemon wedges.

FOOD FOR THOUGHT
Applied gently, grated potato will cool and soothe sunburn. Placed on muslin, it can soothe and calm the delicate tissues around the eye area. This will give the eyes an instant lift.

HEALTH BENEFITS
Potatoes yield protein and are an excellent source of vitamins A and C. They are said to contain cancer inhibitors, and the potassium found in potatoes may help prevent high blood pressure and strokes.

celeriac fish soup with sage crostini

The combination of bread, fish and sage can be traced back to biblical times. This recipe evokes a sense of the Mediterranean.

SERVES 8

1 sourdough baguette (yesterday's bread)
150ml extra-virgin olive oil
6 fresh sage leaves, finely chopped or 1 flat
  tsp dried sage
Salt and freshly ground black pepper
4 tbsp olive oil
200g celeriac, peeled and finely diced
1 medium red onion, finely diced
1 large potato, peeled and finely diced

3 cloves garlic, peeled and crushed
3 bay leaves
1 star anise
4 large tomatoes, peeled and chopped
1 tbsp capers
1 cup white wine
1½ litres fish or vegetable stock
400g smoked snapper
400g snapper fillets, cut into 1cm slices

Pre-heat oven to 170°C. To make crostini, slice baguette into long, thin ovals and place on a baking tray. Gently warm extra-virgin olive oil in a saucepan. Add sage, stir well and cool. Lavishly brush bread with oil and sage mixture; season with salt and pepper. Bake in oven for 10 minutes until golden-brown. Set aside to cool.

Place a large, heavy-based pot on medium heat. Add second measure of olive oil, celeriac, onion and potato. Stirring continuously, cook until onion is transparent. Add garlic, bay leaves, star anise, tomatoes and capers. Cook for 5 minutes. Add wine and cook for a further 3 minutes. Add stock, bring to boil and reduce to simmer for 10 minutes.

Using your hands, gently remove and discard the skin and bones from smoked snapper. Break fish into small flakes and drop into soup. Simmer for 5 minutes. Add sliced snapper fillets to soup. Simmer for a further 5 minutes and season with salt and pepper. Serve soup into bowls and top with crostini.

FOOD FOR THOUGHT

Sage (meaning 'to heal') is often documented as the herb of longevity. Ancient druids believed that eating sage leaves improved memory and wisdom. The Greeks believed sage could bestow immortality and the Egyptians regarded it as the giver and saver of life.

HEALTH BENEFITS

Sage is used to counteract excessive sweating. Sage tea is often referred to as the 'menopause tea' to relieve hot flushes and night sweats. It has antiseptic, anti-fungal and anti-inflammatory properties. Used as a gargle, a weak infusion will relieve sore throats, mouth ulcers and sore gums. Sage also helps heal wounds and fight salmonella, and it is an excellent digestive aid. Used as a rinse, a sage infusion will help clear dandruff and bring life to dull grey hair.

funky calamari on atami chinese greens

Hotheads will become addicted to the instant heat of this calamari dish, which retreats as quickly as it appears. The combination of wasabi powder and flour is inspirational. Adjust quantities to suit personal taste. This is delicious served with Japanese sake.

SERVES 4

5 tbsp olive oil
1 heaped tsp cracked black pepper
4 cloves garlic, peeled and crushed
1 large salad bowl Chinese greens,
   roughly sliced
4 tbsp tamari or light soy sauce

1 lemon (finely chopped zest and juice)
50g flour
1 tbsp Japanese wasabi powder
500g calamari (squid tubes), cleaned
Olive oil for frying
1 lemon, cut into wedges, for garnish

Place a large wok on medium heat. Add 4 tablespoons olive oil, pepper and garlic. Cook for 1 minute. Add Chinese greens, tossing continually for 4 minutes. Add tamari, lemon zest and juice. Place mixture onto serving plates. Combine flour and wasabi powder and set aside. Cut calamari into 1cm rings and dust with flour and wasabi mixture. Place a large, heavy-based frying pan on medium heat with just enough olive oil to cover base of pan. Add calamari and cook for 3–4 minutes until rings start to brown. Serve on top of Chinese greens and garnish with lemon wedges.

FOOD FOR THOUGHT

Tamari is a naturally brewed soy sauce that contains no wheat. It has a very strong salty, savoury taste, which can be diluted with water. Wasabi is the Japanese version of horseradish. The green paste served with sushi is wasabi powder mixed with water.

spiced terakihi fillets with slow-roasted tomatoes

Chickpea flour contributes a crisp texture and rich golden colour to the spiced fillets, adding a new dimension to this fish dish.

SERVES 4

3 tbsp brown sugar
1 tsp turmeric
6 firm medium tomatoes, halved
1 lemon (chopped zest and juice)
3 carrots, grated
½ cup roughly chopped fresh coriander
2 tbsp lightly roasted sesame seeds

Salt
600g terakihi fillets, cut into 75g pieces
100g chickpea or pea flour
1 tbsp ground cumin
1 tbsp medium curry powder
4 tbsp olive oil

Pre-heat oven to 110°C. Combine sugar and turmeric in a bowl and mix well. Place tomatoes on a baking tray and sprinkle with the sugar and turmeric mixture. Bake for 1 hour. In a large bowl, combine lemon zest and juice, carrots, coriander and sesame seeds. Season with salt and turn out onto plates to form a bed for fish. Season terakihi with salt. Combine flour, cumin and curry powder. Dust fillets with the dry mixture. Place a heavy-based frying pan on medium heat and add olive oil. Pan-fry fish until golden-brown on both sides. Serve on the carrot mixture with the slow-roasted tomatoes.

HEALTH BENEFITS

Chickpeas were once believed to be an aphrodisiac. Nowadays we know them for their nutritional properties. Chickpeas give the body energy and are high in protein and fibre. Chickpea flour is gluten-free and is a good alternative to ordinary flour. Pea flour is also gluten-free and high in protein.

fast & furious

roasted pumpkin tofu salad

prav's indian tofu

tofu vegetable stir-fry

marinated tofu and sesame sauce stir-fry

tofu scramble

tempeh tandoori stir-fry

tempeh cauliflower with peanut butter

tempeh scramble

roasted pumpkin tofu salad

Pumpkin, especially roasted, is a comfort food and is very good for you. The cucumber and lemon in this salad act as a refreshing palate-cleanser.

SERVES 4

6 tbsp olive oil
2 blocks firm tofu, each cut lengthwise into 2 slices through middle
4 tbsp tamari or light soy sauce
1 medium green butternut pumpkin
Salt and freshly ground black pepper
½ cup lightly roasted pumpkin seeds
1 cos lettuce, cut into 3cm slices

1 telegraph cucumber, cut lengthways, quartered, de-seeded and cut into 1cm angled slices
1 lemon (chopped zest and juice)
¼ cup roughly chopped fresh mint
¼ cup finely sliced spring onions
2 tbsp roasted sesame oil
1 large avocado, sliced, for garnish

Pre-heat oven to 175°C. Put 4 tablespoons olive oil in a heavy-based frying pan on medium heat. Add tofu and cook for approximately 2 minutes per side until golden-brown. Drain on paper towels. Place tofu on flat plate and spoon 1 tablespoon tamari over each slice. Leave in tamari for 1 minute, then turn slices over and cool. Remove tofu from plate, cut into 2cm cubes and return cubes to tamari. Set aside. De-seed pumpkin, cut into 3cm cubes (leave skin on) and toss in 2 tablespoons olive oil. Season with salt and pepper, place in roasting tray and bake for 30 minutes. Remove from oven and cool.

In a large bowl, combine tofu, pumpkin cubes, pumpkin seeds, cos lettuce, cucumber, lemon zest and juice, mint, spring onions and sesame oil. Spoon salad into bowls and garnish with sliced avocado.

FOOD FOR THOUGHT

Don't throw pumpkin seeds away — wash them thoroughly and roast on a baking tray until dry. Spray on a little olive oil and toast for a further 5 minutes. Remove from oven, sprinkle with salt and cool. Roasted pumpkin seeds taste great in sandwiches or added to your favourite salad.

HEALTH BENEFITS

Pumpkins, a member of the gourd family, are low in calories, rich in minerals and high in beta-carotene and other carotenoids. Pumpkin is kind to delicate stomachs and the seeds are a good source of essential fatty acids and vitamins.

prav's indian tofu

Every time someone asks 'What do you do with tofu?', I suggest this recipe. It is simple and savoury and has interesting textures — all the things that people say tofu lacks. Adjust the amount of chilli to suit your taste.

SERVES 4

2 tbsp olive oil
2 large onions, diced
2 blocks firm tofu (crumble, place in tea-towel and wring moisture out)
2 cloves garlic, peeled and crushed

½ tsp turmeric
1 tsp ground cumin
2 chillies, finely chopped
½ cup roughly chopped fresh coriander
1 cup finely sliced and blanched spinach

Place a heavy-based frying pan on medium heat. Add olive oil and onions and cook until onion is transparent. Add tofu, garlic, turmeric and cumin and cook for 5 minutes. When tofu sticks to pan, use a wooden spoon to gently work it free. Toss ingredients in pan continually. Add chillies and coriander. Sprinkle spinach over mixture and serve on freshly cooked basmati rice.

FOOD FOR THOUGHT

Coriander is widely used in many Indian dishes and is recognised for its medicinal properties. Crushed and roasted coriander seeds mixed with warm water make a gargle that is said to help cure thrush in the mouth.

HEALTH BENEFITS

Coriander is well known as a digestive aid. It can help to prevent infection and kill bacteria. Coriander's anti-inflammatory properties may help sufferers of arthritis.

tofu vegetable stir-fry

This dish surely qualifies as an everyday favourite. It combines simplicity with great taste and texture. The recipe is very adaptable and you can use whatever vegetables you have available.

SERVES 4

2 tbsp olive oil
1 block firm tofu, cubed 2cm
1 onion, sliced
1 tsp cumin seeds
1 head of broccoli, cut into flowerets
2 courgettes, cut in half lengthways, then into 2cm slices

1 tbsp ginger paste
1 red pepper, thinly sliced
2 tbsp lightly roasted sesame seeds
2 tbsp tamari or light soy sauce
½ cup vegetable stock
½ cup finely sliced spring onions

Place a large wok on high heat. Add olive oil and tofu. Toss tofu until surface begins to brown. Add onion and cumin and cook until onion is transparent. Add broccoli, courgettes, ginger and red pepper. Cook for 2 minutes. Add sesame seeds, tamari and vegetable stock. Cover wok and cook for a further 2 minutes. Add spring onions and toss. Serve on freshly cooked rice.

FOOD FOR THOUGHT

If a fresh paint smell is affecting your breathing, then this old-fashioned remedy should do the trick. Take two onions and halve them. Place the onion halves at each corner of the room. For some reason the onions absorb the paint smell.

HEALTH BENEFITS

The vitamin C and beta-carotene found in broccoli are useful in the prevention of heart disease. Broccoli is absolutely loaded with antioxidants, and research shows it plays an important role in the fight against breast and colon cancer.

marinated tofu and sesame sauce stir-fry

The sesame seed paste provides the base for this recipe; combined with the savoury depth of tamari, it makes a very satisfying simple dish.

SERVES 4

6 tbsp olive oil
2 blocks firm tofu, each cut lengthwise
  into 2 slices through middle
6 tbsp tamari or light soy sauce
1 cup lightly roasted sesame seeds
4 tbsp water

2 medium carrots, thinly sliced
1 thumb-size piece fresh ginger, cut into
  thin matchsticks
2 cups quartered button mushrooms
1 onion, finely sliced
1 large bowl sliced and mixed Chinese greens

Put 4 tablespoons olive oil in a heavy-based frying pan on medium heat. Add tofu and cook for approximately 2 minutes per side until golden-brown. Drain on paper towels. Place tofu on flat plate and spoon 1 tablespoon tamari over each slice. Leave in tamari for 1 minute, then turn slices over and cool. Remove tofu from plate, cut into 2cm cubes and return cubes to tamari.

Place sesame seeds in blender and grind into fine crumbs. Add 2 tablespoons tamari and the water and pulse until mixture forms a thick paste. Spoon into a container and refrigerate.

Place a large wok on medium heat. Add the remaining 2 tablespoons olive oil, carrots, ginger, mushrooms and onion. Cook for 4 minutes, tossing continually. Add Chinese greens and cook for a further 2 minutes. Add tofu and any remaining tamari. Spoon sesame sauce onto ingredients, toss to combine, cook for 1 minute and serve on freshly cooked rice.

HEALTH BENEFITS

Many eastern cultures use mushrooms as a food and a medicine because they believe mushrooms promote health and longevity. Mushrooms have anti-viral and immune-boosting properties. Shiitake mushrooms, in particular, have been linked with the reduced risk of certain types of cancer. Mushrooms provide the body with a good source of riboflavin and niacin. Riboflavin contributes to healthy skin and eyes. Niacin is important for the healthy function of the digestive and nervous systems of the body.

tofu scramble

The original fast and easy tofu recipe — if you master this one, you will open the door to many satisfying tofu dishes.

SERVES 4

2 tbsp olive oil
1 large onion, diced
2 large carrots, diced
2 celery sticks, diced
2 blocks firm tofu (crumble, place in tea-towel and wring moisture out)

2 courgettes, sliced into rounds
1 tbsp ginger paste
4 tbsp tamari or light soy sauce
½ cup finely sliced spring onions
Fresh coriander leaves for garnish

Place a heavy-based frying pan on medium heat. Add olive oil, onion, carrots and celery. Cook until onion is transparent, then add tofu. When tofu sticks to pan, use a wooden spoon to gently work it free. Tofu will begin to brown and take on the texture of scrambled eggs. Add courgettes and ginger. Cook for a further 4 minutes. Add tamari and spring onions. Toss ingredients in pan, ensuring that tofu remains moist. Serve on top of whole-wheat toast or cooked brown rice. Garnish with coriander leaves.

FOOD FOR THOUGHT
Celery is your best friend if you are watching what you eat and feel the need to snack. Three sticks of celery contain around 25 calories. You will use up more calories actually digesting the celery.

HEALTH BENEFITS
Celery is a popular vegetable and widely used as a herbal remedy. The use of crushed celery seeds in herbal remedies dates back to the 19th century. In addition, celery seeds are known for their diuretic properties and for helping to clear toxins from the body. They also contain a substance that acts as a sedative, excellent for insomniacs. Celery plays an important role in maintaining healthy joints. It is said to be beneficial in the treatment of gout, rheumatism, arthritis and anxiety.

tempeh tandoori stir-fry

Don't be put off by tempeh. Its nutty, savoury flavour is perfect with tandoori paste and coconut cream in this nutritious and substantial dish. The kumara provides a sweet, soft texture.

SERVES 4

5 tbsp olive oil
1 block tempeh, cubed 2cm
2 tsp tandoori curry paste
1 cup coconut cream
Salt
1 tsp caraway seeds
1 large onion, finely sliced
2 medium carrots, cut into matchsticks

1 thumb-size piece of fresh ginger, cut into matchsticks
2 medium kumara or sweet potatoes, cooked and cut into 2cm x 4cm batons
1 cauliflower, cut into flowerets
200g spinach, roughly chopped
½ cup roughly chopped fresh coriander

Put 3 tablespoons olive oil in a heavy-based frying pan on medium heat. Add tempeh and cook until golden-brown. Drain on paper towels and set aside to cool. Combine curry paste and coconut cream. Fold in tempeh and season with salt. Pour remaining olive oil into a large wok on medium heat. Add caraway seeds, onion, carrots and ginger. Cook for 4 minutes, continually tossing ingredients in wok. Add kumara and cauliflower and cook for a further 3 minutes. Add tempeh and spinach and cook for a further 3 minutes, tossing continually. Add coriander and season with salt. Serve on basmati rice spiced with turmeric.

FOOD FOR THOUGHT

Left-over coconut milk makes a lovely bath blend. Just add a few drops of your favourite essential oils to the coconut milk, mix well and add to running bath water. Relaxing and soothing: a two-for-one treat.

HEALTH BENEFITS

Cauliflower, derived from a Latin word meaning 'cabbage flower', belongs to the same plant family as broccoli and cabbage. All contain compounds that are said to inhibit the development of some cancers. Amongst other things, cauliflower is a good source of vitamin C, fibre, folate and potassium. The fibre in cauliflower keeps the bowels happy and healthy.

tempeh cauliflower with peanut butter

Peanut butter and tempeh are fantastic partners, complementing each other with consistent texture and taste. This dish brings the two ingredients together with an Indian-based flavour and uses cauliflower as an ideal base. Good served with basmati rice.

SERVES 4

5 tbsp olive oil
1 block tempeh, cubed 2cm
1 onion, sliced
1 carrot, cut into thin rounds
1 thumb-size piece of ginger, cut into matchsticks
1 tsp ground cumin

1 tsp cumin seeds
1 cauliflower, cut into thin flowerets
2 courgettes, cut into 2cm rounds
4 tbsp crunchy peanut butter
½ cup vegetable stock
½ cup roughly chopped fresh coriander
Salt

Put 2 tablespoons olive oil into a heavy-based frying pan on medium heat. Pan-fry tempeh until golden-brown, then set aside. Place a large wok on medium heat and add the remaining olive oil, onion, carrot, ginger, ground cumin and cumin seeds. Cook until onion is transparent. Add cauliflower and courgettes and cook for a further 5 minutes, continually tossing ingredients. Add peanut butter, vegetable stock, coriander and tempeh, and combine. Season with salt, cook for a further 2 minutes and serve immediately.

FOOD FOR THOUGHT

Leftover ginger makes a nice infusion that will relieve tired aching muscles when added to your bath. Add 3 teaspoons freshly grated ginger to 1½ cups warm water and allow to simmer for 25 minutes. Strain and add to bath. Lie back and relax for about 15 minutes. Ginger helps improve circulation, is very relaxing and brings warmth to cold bodies. Do not use if you suffer from high blood pressure or if you are pregnant.

tempeh scramble

A sister dish to Tofu Scramble (see page 78), with added texture. Tempeh has a superior savoury flavour to tofu.

SERVES 4

2 tbsp olive oil
1 large onion, diced
2 large carrots, diced
2 celery sticks, diced
1 block tempeh, cubed 1cm

2 courgettes, sliced into rounds
1 tbsp ginger paste
4 tbsp tamari or light soy sauce
½ cup finely sliced spring onions
200g spinach, finely sliced

Place a heavy-based frying pan on medium heat. Add olive oil, onion, carrots and celery. Cook until onion is transparent. Add tempeh and cook until golden-brown. Add courgettes and ginger. Cook for a further 4 minutes, then add tamari, spring onions and spinach. Toss ingredients in pan. Tempeh should be moist. Serve on whole-wheat toast or cooked brown rice.

HEALTH BENEFITS

Tempeh is an Indonesian delicacy made from whole soybeans. It has a nutty flavour, is high in protein and is a good source of vitamin B12 and calcium. Tempeh also contains fibre and carbohydrates. It helps boosts the immune system and may help prevent cancer and heart disease.

simple bach snacks

classic lettuce rolls

spicy rollups

miso avocado rolls

tahini and miso corn thinnies

mint and avocado corn thinnies

roasted pumpkin corn thinnies

spanish armada tortilla

coconut basmati rice

miso brown rice

marco polo rice salad

classic lettuce rolls

Seeking sustenance, you stagger back to the bach on a hot summer's day. This recipe provides complete refreshment.

SERVES 4

1 tbsp Vegemite
2 tbsp crunchy peanut butter
2 tbsp mayonnaise
4 leaves iceberg lettuce, chilled
2 large carrots, grated and tossed in lemon juice

¼ cup finely chopped parsley
2 cloves garlic, peeled and crushed
Salt
4 tbsp whole roasted peanuts

Spread Vegemite, peanut butter and mayonnaise on inside of lettuce leaves. Combine carrots, parsley and garlic in a bowl and season with salt. Lay a bed of carrot mixture across the main lettuce-leaf vein close to the stem. Sprinkle peanuts over carrot mixture. Take the lettuce-leaf stem, roll over ingredients and pull slightly back towards you, compressing the mixture to form a roll. Fold sides over and roll up as firmly as possible.

HEALTH BENEFITS

Vegemite is a concentrated yeast extract and a rich source of the B group of vitamins. It is also a good source of folate and niacin. Folate helps make healthy red blood cells. Niacin helps lower cholesterol and is essential to the maintenance of healthy hair and nails. One serving of Vegemite on your toast in the morning provides your body with a large percentage of the B vitamins it requires daily.

spicy rollups

Peanut butter is the special ingredient in these lettuce rolls.

SERVES 4

2 tbsp crunchy peanut butter
2 tbsp mango chutney or similar
4 leaves iceberg lettuce, chilled
2 large carrots, grated and tossed in
   lemon juice

2 chillies, finely diced
2 cloves garlic, peeled and crushed
½ cup roughly chopped fresh coriander
2 tbsp lightly roasted desiccated coconut
Salt

Spread peanut butter and chutney on inside of lettuce leaves. Combine carrots, chillies, garlic, coriander and coconut in a bowl and season with salt. Lay a bed of carrot mixture across the main lettuce-leaf vein close to the stem. Take the lettuce-leaf stem, roll over ingredients and pull slightly back towards you, compressing the mixture to form a roll. Fold sides over and roll up as firmly as possible.

FOOD FOR THOUGHT

Spring onions are much milder than ordinary onions. When chopped, the long, hollow, green tops of spring onions look lovely used as a garnish in soups or salads. Use the hollow green tops in their entirety to decorate vegetable juices.

HEALTH BENEFITS

Spring onions are a source of vitamin C, beta-carotene, small quantities of potassium and calcium.

miso avocado rolls

In this dish, the savoury taste of miso combines with lush avocado to create classic Japanese flavours with a twist.

SERVES 4

1 tbsp miso
4 leaves iceberg lettuce, chilled
1 medium avocado, mashed with a squeeze
   of lemon juice and seasoned with salt
2 cloves garlic, peeled and crushed

4 tbsp mixed sprouts (alfalfa, mung bean,
   radish)
1 tbsp finely sliced spring onions
1 tbsp lightly roasted sesame seeds

Spread miso on inside of lettuce leaves. Combine avocado, garlic, sprouts, spring onions and sesame seeds in a bowl. Lay a bed of avocado mixture across the main lettuce-leaf vein close to the stem. Take the lettuce-leaf stem, roll over ingredients and pull slightly back towards you, compressing the mixture to form a roll. Fold sides over and roll up as firmly as possible.

FOOD FOR THOUGHT

The humble lettuce plays a role in lowering the risk of some cancers, particularly stomach cancer.

HEALTH BENEFITS

Iceberg lettuce is 95 percent water, low in calories, high in fibre and vitamin C, and a good source of antioxidants, iron and folate. Folate, one of the B vitamins, is essential for healthy red blood cells and is said to reduce the risk of birth defects such as spina bifida. Iron helps prevent anaemia. Lettuce is eaten raw, so none of the goodness is lost through cooking.

tahini and miso corn thinnies

The fusion of miso from Japan with tahini from Lebanon works extremely well in this recipe.

SERVES 4

1 tbsp miso
4 x 10cm corn thins (available from any supermarket)
1 tbsp tahini
4 tbsp grated courgette

2 tomatoes, diced
1 clove garlic, peeled and crushed
1 tbsp finely sliced spring onions
Salt

Spread miso onto corn thins. Combine tahini, courgette, tomatoes, garlic and spring onions in a bowl. Mix well and season with salt. Spread mixture onto corn thins and enjoy!

FOOD FOR THOUGHT

Tahini is a sesame seed paste. This versatile ingredient can be used in dressings and sauces. A mixture of tahini, tamari, honey, lemon juice, garlic and vinegar makes a very nice dressing.

HEALTH BENEFITS

Tahini contains high levels of vitamin E, protein, potassium and calcium.

mint and avocado corn thinnies

You might find yourself becoming addicted to thinnies, especially if you have an intolerance to wheat. Invent your own combinations as you please.

SERVES 4

2 tbsp peanut butter
4 x 10cm corn thins (available from any supermarket)
½ medium avocado, mashed with a squeeze of lemon juice

2 tbsp de-seeded and diced cucumber
½ tbsp chopped fresh mint
2 tbsp diced red pepper
Salt and freshly ground black pepper

Spread peanut butter onto corn thins. Combine avocado, cucumber, mint and red pepper in a bowl. Mix well and season with salt and pepper. Spread mixture onto corn thins.

FOOD FOR THOUGHT

Cucumber is an old-fashioned remedy for blemishes. Place leftover cucumber in a blender, liquefy and apply to the face. Frozen, sliced cucumber is good for puffy or irritated eyes.

HEALTH BENEFITS

Cucumbers are known as a light food. Consisting mainly of water, they are low in calories and are good in any healthy eating plan. Their mild diuretic properties help prevent fluid retention.

clockwise from top left:
tahini and miso corn thinnies;
mint and avocado corn thinnies;
roasted pumpkin corn thinnies.

roasted pumpkin corn thinnies

Never underestimate the savoury value of roasted pumpkin; it is terrific combined with garlic, black pepper and tamari sauce.

SERVES 4

1 cup mashed roasted pumpkin
1 medium red onion, finely diced
1 tbsp olive oil
1 clove garlic, peeled and crushed
½ tsp cracked black pepper
1 tbsp tamari or light soy sauce

1 tbsp sliced spring onions
Salt
4 x 10cm corn thins (available from any supermarket)
2 tbsp roasted, roughly chopped and salted pumpkin seeds

Combine pumpkin, onion, olive oil, garlic, pepper, tamari and spring onions in a bowl. Mix well and season with salt. Spread onto corn thins and sprinkle with pumpkin seeds. This is a really cool dairy-free snack. (See photo page 89.)

FOOD FOR THOUGHT

Did you know that the word pumpkin is derived from the Greek word, pepon, meaning large melon?

HEALTH BENEFITS

Tasty pumpkin seeds provide energy and are a useful source of iron and zinc. Zinc supports the immune system and helps the body fight infection. Pumpkin seeds are said to help men suffering from prostate problems.

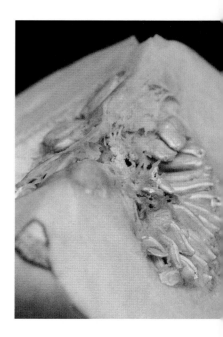

spanish armada tortilla

Tortilla breads are great fun — you can adapt the fillings to your own taste and they are great to take on holiday. Make sure the tortilla bread is fresh. Warm it gently in the oven before filling and rolling.

SERVES 4

4 tbsp olive oil
4 medium potatoes, peeled, cooked whole
   until firm to centre and cubed 1.5cm
1 tsp Spanish paprika
4 cloves garlic, peeled and crushed
2 red onions, finely diced
Salt and freshly ground black pepper
½ cup chopped fresh coriander
½ cup lightly roasted almond slices

4 round flour tortillas, 24cm or 26cm
1 iceberg lettuce, very finely sliced, placed in
   cold water with juice of 1 lemon
4 tomatoes, diced
½ cup natural yoghurt
1 cup grated cheddar cheese
2 large just-ripe avocados, cut into long
   thin slices

Pre-heat oven to 170°C. Place a large frying pan on medium heat. Add olive oil, potatoes, paprika and garlic. Cook until potatoes start to brown. Add onions. Season with salt and pepper. Cook for a further 2 minutes. Turn out into a bowl, add coriander and almonds, mix well and set aside.

Heat tortillas in oven for 3–4 minutes. Remove and lay on flat surface. Drain enough lettuce (dry on paper or tea-towel) to lay a thick bed across the centre of each tortilla. Spoon warm potato mixture along lettuce. Add tomatoes, yoghurt, cheese and avocados. Season with salt and pepper. Take the edge of the tortilla nearest to you, lay it over filling and pull slightly back towards you, compressing the mixture to form a roll. Now, fold over the other side of the tortilla and roll up as firmly as possible. Eat immediately.

FOOD FOR THOUGHT

Almonds make lovely milk, for which you need ½ cup chopped almonds, 2 cups water, ½ teaspoon vanilla and 4 tablespoons runny honey. Blend almonds with 1 cup water for 4 minutes. Add second cup of water, blend and add vanilla and honey. Strain liquid through muslin into a glass bowl. Squeeze muslin tightly to ensure you have extracted as much milk as possible. This is a fantastic drink for the lactose intolerant. What is left in the muslin can be used as a face or body scrub. That's 'two for the price of one'.

HEALTH BENEFITS

Almonds are a very good source of protein and mono-unsaturated fats, calcium and vitamin E. Eating a handful of almonds a day may lower what we often refer to as 'bad' cholesterol and reduce the risk of heart disease.

coconut basmati rice

Making the most of leftover basmati rice, this is a quick, light, moreish and savoury dish.

SERVES 4

4 tbsp olive oil
1 red onion, diced
1 carrot, diced
1 tsp cumin seeds
2 cloves garlic, peeled and crushed

4 cups basmati rice, cooked, cooled and refrigerated overnight
½ cup roughly chopped fresh coriander
½ cup lightly roasted coconut threads
Salt

Place a wok on medium heat. Add olive oil, onion, carrot, cumin and garlic. Cook until onion is transparent. Add rice and cook for 4 minutes. Continually turn rice with a wooden spoon to prevent it sticking to the wok. Add coriander and coconut. Cook for a further 2 minutes. Season with salt and serve.

FOOD FOR THOUGHT

In folklore, rice is associated with fertility. For that reason, it is thrown at newly wed couples as they emerge from their place of worship. In some countries, such as China and Japan, most meals would not be complete without rice. In India, basmati rice is used more often in ceremonial dishes. It has a lovely aromatic fragrance and fresh taste.

HEALTH BENEFITS

Rice, a staple food in many modern homes, contains starch and fibre. Fibre keeps the bowel healthy. Rice is gluten-free, easily digestible and hypoallergenic.

top: miso brown rice,
bottom: coconut basmati rice.

miso brown rice

An absolute favourite of mine, this dish can be eaten for breakfast, lunch or dinner.

SERVES 4

2 tbsp olive oil
1 onion, diced
1 carrot, finely diced
1 block firm tofu, cubed 2cm
1 tbsp ginger paste
1 tbsp miso
½ cup vegetable stock

1 tbsp tamari or light soy sauce
4 cups brown rice, cooked, cooled and
    refrigerated overnight
200g spinach, finely sliced
½ cup finely sliced spring onions
1 tbsp lightly roasted sesame seeds

Place a heavy-based frying pan on medium heat. Add olive oil, onion, carrot and tofu. Cook until onion is transparent. Add ginger and miso. Cook for a further 3 minutes. Add vegetable stock, tamari, rice and spinach. Combine thoroughly. Add spring onions, sprinkle with sesame seeds and serve. (See photo page 93.)

FOOD FOR THOUGHT
Miso is a thick paste made from fermented soybeans. It is used to flavour many culinary dishes, including soups and casseroles.

HEALTH BENEFITS
Miso aids digestion and metabolism. It is jam-packed with protein and is a good source of the B vitamins. Japanese culture believes that miso is vital for good health and long life. It improves the body's resistance to illness and, taken in the form of a drink, is said to reduce irritability and boost energy levels.

marco polo rice salad

A salad that represents a fusion of ingredients from different cuisine styles, named after adventurer Marco Polo.

SERVES 4

4 cups sushi rice, cooked and cooled
2 tbsp umeboshi or brown rice vinegar
1 just-ripe avocado, diced
1 block silken tofu, cubed 2cm
½ cup lightly roasted pine nuts
½ cup sliced spring onions
2 tbsp roasted sesame seeds
2 cups blanched and finely sliced spinach

1 head of broccoli, cut into flowerets
  and blanched
2 tbsp tamari or light soy sauce

DRESSING
1 lemon (chopped zest and juice)
3 tbsp olive oil
1 tbsp tamari or light soy sauce

In a large bowl, combine rice and umeboshi. In another large bowl, combine avocado, tofu, pine nuts, spring onions, sesame seeds, spinach, broccoli and tamari. Set aside. Place rice in serving bowls and spoon vegetable mixture over rice.

To make dressing, combine lemon zest and juice, olive oil and tamari in a jar, cover and shake well. Pour dressing over rice and vegetables.

FOOD FOR THOUGHT

If you cut yourself when cooking, don't panic. Simply squeeze some lemon juice onto the cut. The bad news . . . it will sting. The good news . . . it will stem the bleeding and act as an antiseptic.

bbq summer foods

paprika and mushroom pita

kumara, caper and parmesan pita

curried spinach pita

apricot tofu kebabs

garlic manis tofu kebabs

plum and tempeh kebabs

paprika and mushroom pita

A fast food for summer, this dish uses a simple yet effective combination of paprika, mushrooms, garlic and white wine refreshed with lettuce and tomato — and a savoury mix of cheese, onion and parsley.

SERVES 4

4 tbsp olive oil
1 large red onion, diced
1 large carrot, diced
4 cloves garlic, peeled and crushed
2 cups sliced mushrooms
1½ tsp paprika
½ cup white wine

Salt and freshly ground black pepper
4 x 22cm pita breads
½ iceberg lettuce, finely sliced
2 large tomatoes, diced
½ cup grated cheddar cheese
½ cup finely chopped parsley

Put 3 tablespoons olive oil in a heavy-based frying pan on medium heat. Add onion, carrot, garlic and mushrooms and cook for 4 minutes. Add 1 teaspoon paprika and the wine. Cook for a further 4 minutes. Season with salt and pepper, remove from pan and place in a large bowl. Set aside. Combine the remaining olive oil and paprika. Cut pita breads in half and brush inside and out with the oil and paprika mixture. Toast pita breads on a barbecue, hot plate or grill. Half-fill each hot pita bread with lettuce, then add mushroom mixture and tomatoes. Sprinkle cheddar and parsley on top. Serve hot. (See photo page 99.)

FOOD FOR THOUGHT

Parsley makes a lovely hair tonic. Place 1 cup parsley and 4 tablespoons water in a blender. Blend until you have a smooth liquid. Apply to dry hair and scalp, wrap in cling wrap and place a warm towel over cling wrap. Leave tonic to penetrate for 40 minutes. Remove towel and cling wrap. Shampoo as usual. Parsley stimulates the scalp and when your hair is dry it will look lovely and shiny.

HEALTH BENEFITS

Cheese provides one of the best sources of calcium. Calcium is vital for strong bones and healthy teeth. Paprika is wonderful for stimulating the appetite.

kumara, caper and parmesan pita

This dish is a Kiwi-Mediterranean combination, wrapped in Lebanese bread. The kumara-caper fusion is an interesting one and I suggest you be generous with the basil and pumpkin seeds.

SERVES 4

2 medium kumara or sweet potatoes
4 tbsp olive oil
1 large red onion, diced
1 large carrot, diced
1 cup French beans, cut into 5mm rounds
4 cloves garlic, peeled and crushed
½ cup white wine

1 tbsp capers
1 tbsp roughly chopped fresh basil
Salt and freshly ground black pepper
½ cup finely grated Parmesan cheese
4 x 22cm pita breads
½ iceberg lettuce, finely sliced
½ cup lightly roasted pumpkin seeds

Cook kumara whole and set aside to cool. Place a heavy-based frying pan on medium heat. Add 3 tablespoons olive oil, onion and carrot. Cook for 4 minutes. Peel and dice kumara and add to pan with beans and 3 of the garlic cloves. Cook for a further 4 minutes. Add wine, capers and basil. Season with salt and pepper. Remove from pan, place in a large bowl, fold in Parmesan and set aside. Combine the remaining olive oil and garlic. Cut pita breads in half and brush inside and out with the oil and garlic mixture. Toast pita breads on a barbecue, hot plate or grill. Half-fill each hot pita bread with lettuce, then add kumara mixture. Sprinkle pumpkin seeds on top. Serve hot.

HEALTH BENEFITS

Basil not only adds flavour to your food, it also helps indigestion, stimulates the immune system and helps fight infection. Fresh basil rubbed on insect bites may reduce inflammation. Basil is also said to help reduce stress and clear the mind.

from left: kumara, caper and parmesan pita; paprika and mushroom pita; curried spinach pita

curried spinach pita

The combination of spinach, curry, ginger and coconut cream gives this dish a wow factor. Be adventurous and add some finely diced fresh chilli.

SERVES 4

4 tbsp olive oil
1 large onion, diced
1 tbsp cumin seeds
1½ tbsp medium curry powder
1 large red pepper, diced
1 tbsp ginger paste
2 medium courgettes, diced

200g spinach, finely sliced
½ cup coconut cream
Salt and freshly ground black pepper
½ cup roughly chopped fresh coriander
4 x 22cm pita breads
½ iceberg lettuce, finely sliced

Place a heavy-based frying pan on medium heat. Add 3 tablespoons olive oil, onion and cumin. Cook for 4 minutes. Add 1 tablespoon curry powder, red pepper, ginger and courgettes. Cook for a further 4 minutes. Add spinach and coconut cream; season with salt and pepper. Remove from pan, place in a large bowl and fold in coriander. Set aside. Combine the remaining olive oil and curry powder. Cut pita breads in half and brush inside and out with the oil and curry mixture. Toast pita breads on a barbecue, hot plate or grill. Half-fill each hot pita bread with lettuce, then add curried spinach mixture. Serve hot. (See photo page 99.)

FOOD FOR THOUGHT

Make a conditioning lotion that will work wonders on your hair. Mix leftover coconut cream with a mashed avocado until you have a thick, shampoo-like mixture. Comb or massage through dry hair and cover your head with cling wrap. Leave to penetrate hair for 20 minutes. Wash hair thoroughly.

apricot tofu kebabs

A combination of sweet, spicy and savoury tastes to seduce and satisfy.

SERVES 4

5 tbsp olive oil
2 blocks firm tofu, cubed 3cm
1 large red onion, quartered
1 large carrot, sliced into 5mm rounds
1 large red pepper, sliced into 3cm triangles
8 large firm apricots, de-stoned and quartered

8 wooden skewers, soaked in water for 1 hour
1 tbsp green curry paste
2 tbsp water
1 tbsp maple syrup
1 tbsp rice wine
Salt and freshly ground black pepper

Place a heavy-based frying pan on medium heat. Add 4 tablespoons olive oil and fry tofu until golden-brown. Drain and cool tofu on paper towels. Spike tofu, onion, carrot, red pepper and apricots onto skewers. Combine curry paste, water, maple syrup, rice wine and the remaining olive oil. Coat kebabs thickly with curry mixture, reserving some mixture for serving. Season with salt and pepper and leave to stand for 5 minutes. Cook on a barbecue, hot plate or grill, rotating skewers to ensure ingredients cook evenly and edges are golden-brown. Cover kebabs with remaining curry mixture and serve. (See photo page 103.)

HEALTH BENEFITS

Apricots provide the body with potassium, beta-carotene and soluble fibre. They have antioxidant properties that are known to fight some degenerative illnesses. The soluble fibre found in apricots is said to slow the digestion process, thus providing the body with a more sustainable flow of energy.

garlic manis tofu kebabs

These kebabs deliver a big savoury taste with the combination of kécap manis sauce, garlic, cracked black pepper and mushrooms. A good recipe to prepare ahead of time.

SERVES 4

4 tbsp olive oil
2 blocks firm tofu, cubed 3cm
1 large red onion, quartered
1 large green pepper, sliced into 3cm triangles
1 large carrot, sliced into 5mm rounds
16 medium-sized button mushrooms

8 wooden skewers, soaked in water for 1 hour
4 cloves garlic, peeled and crushed
4 tbsp kécap manis sauce
4 tbsp olive oil
1 tsp cracked black pepper

Place a heavy-based frying pan on medium heat. Add olive oil and fry tofu until golden-brown. Drain and cool tofu on paper towels. Spike tofu, onion, green pepper, carrot and mushrooms onto skewers. Combine garlic, manis sauce, second measure of olive oil and cracked black pepper. Coat kebabs thickly with manis mixture, reserving some mixture for serving. Leave to stand for 5 minutes. Cook on a barbecue, hot plate or grill, rotating skewers to ensure ingredients cook evenly and edges are golden-brown. Cover kebabs with remaining manis mixture and serve.

FOOD FOR THOUGHT

If you have difficulty peeling garlic cloves, simply zap them in the oven at 150°C for 5 minutes and the skin should slip right off the clove. To remove the smell of garlic from your fingers, hold a spoon between your hands and run cold water over them. The smell should just disappear down the drain.

from left: apricot tofu kebabs;
plum and tempeh kebabs; garlic manis tofu kebabs.

plum and tempeh kebabs

This recipe will win you over with little surprises. Once pan-fried, the tempeh yields an enticing gold colour and a savoury, crunchy texture. The plums are sweet and the spike of red curry paste can be tasted through the coconut cream.

SERVES 4

4 tbsp olive oil
2 blocks tempeh, cubed 3cm
1 large red onion, quartered
8 large firm plums, de-stoned and quartered
1 large carrot, sliced into 5mm rounds
2 large courgettes, sliced into 1cm rounds

8 wooden skewers, soaked in water for 1 hour
²/₃ cup coconut cream
1 tsp red curry paste
Salt and freshly ground black pepper
½ cup roughly chopped fresh coriander

Place a heavy-based frying pan on medium heat. Add olive oil and fry tempeh until golden-brown. Drain and cool tempeh on paper towels. Spike tempeh, onion, plums, carrot and courgettes onto skewers. Combine coconut cream and curry paste. Coat kebabs thickly with coconut sauce, reserving some sauce for serving. Season with salt and pepper and leave to stand for 5 minutes. Cook on a barbecue, hot plate or grill, rotating skewers to ensure ingredients cook evenly and edges are golden-brown. Cover kebabs with remaining coconut sauce, sprinkle with coriander and serve. (See photo page 103.)

HEALTH BENEFITS

Plums are a natural laxative. Dried plums (such as prunes) contain potassium, vitamin A, magnesium, iron and fibre. They are high in antioxidants, which play an important role in the ageing process and the prevention of certain cancers and heart conditions.

sweet dreams

doris plum and honey cheesecake

chocolate cherry hazelnut cake

star anise apple bran crumble

strawberry sweethearts

lemon and pear flan

melon and mint sorbet

cashew and rhubarb delight

doris plum and honey cheesecake

The soft smooth texture of Black Doris plums is just perfect matched with the gingernut base of this divine cheesecake.

SERVES 8

BASE
½ packet wine biscuits
½ packet gingernuts
½ cup plain flour
2 heaped tbsp honey
½ cup cold-pressed sunflower oil

FILLING
4 eggs
250g sour cream
1 tsp almond essence
1 lemon (finely chopped zest and juice)
375g cream cheese
225g castor sugar
½ cup plain flour
14 canned Black Doris plums (remove stones and reserve 4 tablespoons juice)

To make the base, place wine biscuits and gingernuts in a food processor. Grind to fine crumbs. Add flour, mix thoroughly and set aside. Place a small saucepan on medium heat. Add honey and oil and heat gently for 5 minutes. Pour into biscuit mixture and combine thoroughly, using pulse button on the food processor. Gently press mixture into the base of a 24cm cheesecake tin and set aside.

Pre-heat oven to 170°C. Separate 3 eggs and set aside the egg whites. In a large mixing bowl, place 3 egg yolks, 1 whole egg, sour cream, almond essence, lemon zest and juice. Mix thoroughly and set aside. In another mixing bowl, combine cream cheese and 120g castor sugar. Sprinkle flour in. Combine cream cheese mixture with the egg and sour cream mixture. Whisk egg whites until they have soft white peaks. Whisk the remaining sugar into the egg whites. Fold egg whites into cheesecake mixture. Pour over base in tin. Bake for 30 minutes.

Remove from oven and space plums evenly across the cheesecake, gently pushing them in. Drizzle plum juice around the edges and across the top of cheesecake. Return to oven and bake for a further 60 minutes until golden-brown. Cool before removing from tin.

FOOD FOR THOUGHT

Sunflower oil will heal and soothe dry, scaly skin. 'Cold-pressed' oil retains the natural ingredients found in the original seed or fruit.

HEALTH BENEFITS

Using cold-pressed sunflower oil instead of cooking fat in recipes is kind to the heart and the liver. Cold-pressed sunflower oil is high in linoleic acid. Research shows that a diet incorporating oils that contain linoleic acid helps to lower cholesterol.

chocolate cherry hazelnut cake

Moist, mouth-watering, delicious, decadent ... What more can I say?!
Well-whisked egg whites are essential to this recipe, as are gentleness
and efficiency when folding the whites into the mixture.

SERVES 8

ICING
350ml cream
250g dark chocolate, crumbled

CAKE
250g dark chocolate
180g unsalted butter
180g brown sugar
7 eggs, separated and set aside
120g hazelnuts, finely ground
120g canned cherries, drained

Make icing 24 hours ahead. Pour cream into a small saucepan on medium heat. Slowly bring to the boil. Reduce heat and add crumbled chocolate. Stir continuously until chocolate melts and is absorbed into cream. Pour mixture into a clean bowl, cool and refrigerate overnight. Remove from fridge before you begin to bake the cake.

Pre-heat oven to 175°C. Melt the second measure of chocolate in a bowl over hot water, then set aside to cool. Cream butter and sugar in a bowl. Add egg yolks one at a time, mixing ingredients continuously until silky and smooth. Add hazelnuts and melted chocolate, which should just be warm. Mix thoroughly. Add cherries and set aside. Whip egg whites until they have soft peaks. Gently fold into chocolate hazelnut mixture. Pour mixture into two 20cm cake tins lined with greaseproof paper. Bake for 35 minutes or until cake looks slightly cracked on surface.

Remove from oven and cool for 30 minutes. You may need to warm the prepared icing gently. Turn one cake out onto a cake plate. Completely cover the surface of the first cake with icing. Turn out second cake and place on top of first cake. Cover the top and sides of the cake with icing. Store in a sealed container; do not refrigerate.

FOOD FOR THOUGHT
Hazelnuts contain vitamin E. Place leftover
hazelnuts in blender and grind finely. Add
ground hazelnuts to your favourite body
wash and you have a simple but effective
body scrub.

star anise apple bran crumble

The star anise adds a distinctive licorice aroma to the humble crumble. The slightly chewy texture of the plums on top makes this bake simply delicious.

SERVES 8

TOPPING
2 cups bran flakes
1 cup brown sugar
1 cup plain flour
1 cup rolled oats
170g unsalted butter, melted

CRUMBLE
60ml water
100g castor sugar
10 large Granny Smith apples, cored, peeled
  and sliced 2cm
2 star anise
¾ cup currants
12 canned Black Doris plums, drained

Pre-heat oven to 175°C. In a large bowl, combine bran, brown sugar, flour and oats. Pour in melted butter, mix thoroughly and set aside.

Place a large saucepan on medium heat. Add water, castor sugar, apples and star anise. Cover and cook for 5 minutes. Add currants, replace cover and reduce heat to low. Cook gently for 15 minutes. Remove from heat and spoon filling into a 30cm x 30cm baking dish. Add topping and compress gently to seal crumble. Arrange plums on top. Bake for 40 minutes. Note: the star anise are for flavour and aroma, not for consumption.

HEALTH BENEFITS
*Apples are a good source of potassium.
Amongst other things, potassium is an essential
mineral for healthy tissues. Potassium is also
referred to as the artery cleanser. So if you want
to keep your skin and muscle tone in good
condition, pay attention to the old saying:
'an apple a day keeps the doctor away'.*

strawberry sweethearts

A delectable shortbread treat for Valentine's Day, served with sliced strawberries and wickedly rich mascarpone cheese.

MAKES 24 BISCUITS

200g unsalted butter, softened
180g icing sugar
4 eggs
1 tsp vanilla essence
280g plain flour

1 heart-shaped biscuit-cutter, 8–10 cm wide
1 punnet ripe strawberries, sliced
75g castor sugar
250g mascarpone cheese
200ml cream, whipped

Pre-heat oven to 170°C. Cream butter in a food processor. Sift icing sugar in and blend thoroughly. Separate 2 eggs, discard whites. Add 2 yolks and vanilla essence to food processor and mix lightly. Sift flour into mixture. Pulse until dough is formed. Wrap dough in cling film and refrigerate for at least 2 hours. Roll dough out onto a cold floured surface until 5mm thick. Cut out heart-shaped biscuits and lay on a greased baking tray. Bake for 12 minutes until lightly golden. Remove from oven and set aside.

Place strawberries in a bowl and sprinkle with 25g castor sugar. Set aside. Separate the remaining 2 eggs and reserve whites. Place yolks in a glass bowl and add the remaining castor sugar. Half-fill a saucepan with water, place on medium heat and bring to boil. Place the glass bowl containing egg yolks over the boiling water and whisk until they have a custard-like consistency. Place mascarpone into a large bowl and stir in egg and sugar mixture. Whisk egg whites into soft peaks and fold into mascaparone mixture. Finally, fold in cream and strawberries. Sandwich biscuits together with a thick filling of strawberry cream.

HEALTH BENEFITS

The sweet and wholesome strawberry is a good source of fibre and antioxidant properties in the form of vitamin C. Believe it or not, strawberries are also noted for their diuretic properties.

lemon and pear flan

During baking, the almonds rise to give a crispy texture to the top of the flan. This recipe is excellent for feeding a crowd; it can be stored in the fridge and makes a great picnic food.

SERVES 10

PASTRY
250g plain flour
80g icing sugar
1 lemon (finely chopped zest and juice)
½ vanilla bean, split
120g unsalted butter, diced
1 egg, whisked

FILLING
500g castor sugar
60ml water
8 large pears, peeled, cored and cut
  into 1cm slices
250g butter
200g almonds, finely ground
3 eggs
1 lemon (finely chopped zest)

Pre-heat oven to 160°C. Sift flour and icing sugar together and add lemon zest. Scrape in seeds from vanilla bean. Add butter, egg and lemon juice; mix using fingertips until a dough is formed. Wrap dough in cling film and refrigerate for at least 2 hours. Roll dough out on a cold floured surface until 5mm thick. Lay in a greased 28cm flan tin. Return to fridge for 30 minutes. Bake for 15 minutes.

Preheat oven to 180°C. To make filling, place 300g castor sugar and the water in a saucepan wide enough to hold the pears in a single layer. Bring sugar and water to boil, stirring until sugar has dissolved. Boil rapidly without stirring until syrup begins to darken, shake pan gently and reduce heat when it turns a light caramel colour. Slowly add pears and cook until they can be pierced easily with a sharp knife. Remove from heat and cool for 10 minutes.

Cream the remaining castor sugar and the butter. Mix in almonds. Whisk eggs for 30 seconds and add to mixture. Add 30ml of syrup from the pears. Pour into pastry shell until two-thirds full, then layer pears in the mixture until the shell is completely full. Mix lemon zest into the remaining pear syrup and pour over flan. Bake for 40 minutes. Cool for 1 hour before slicing and serving.

FOOD FOR THOUGHT
For a relaxing bath, try this: pop zest of 2 lemons into a bowl, add 1 cup Epsom salts and 3 drops of your favourite essential oil. Set aside for 24 hours to allow zest and essential oils to completely absorb into salts. Add to bath, relax and enjoy.

melon and mint sorbet

Sorbets are great fun to create. Once you've mastered the technique, the possible combinations are endless. An ice-cream maker does make it a little easier but it is entirely possible to make sorbet by hand.

SERVES 8

100g castor sugar
500ml honeydew melon purée
100g powdered glucose

2 tbsp finely chopped fresh mint
Fresh mint leaves for garnish

Whisk castor sugar into melon purée. Place glucose in a bowl and melt over hot water. Stir into purée. Sprinkle chopped mint into mixture. Place in an ice-cream machine and follow instructions for making sorbet. Serve using an ice-cream ball scoop and garnish with mint leaves.

To make the sorbet by hand, place the sorbet mixture in a suitable bowl and freeze. Over the next 3 hours, remove sorbet 6 or 7 times and whisk thoroughly to remove iciness before returning sorbet to freezer. It will take approximately 6 hours to freeze the sorbet firm.

HEALTH BENEFITS
Way back in the 12th century, Wilafried of Strabo said, 'If any man can name all the properties of mint, he must know how many fish swim in the Indian Ocean.' Folklore describes mint as useful for indigestion problems, reducing nausea and combating travel sickness.

cashew and rhubarb delight

A simple, versatile recipe that makes a delicious dessert or a sweet temptation for morning tea. Cashews add a welcome nutty texture. Serve with strong black coffee.

SERVES 8

400g sweet shortcrust pastry, thawed
500g rhubarb, chopped
¼ cup water

½ cup castor sugar
2 tbsp finely sliced preserved ginger
¾ cup roughly ground cashew nuts

Pre-heat oven to 175°C. Roll pastry out and lay in a greased 24cm pie dish. Bake for 10 minutes. Remove from oven and set aside.

Place a large saucepan on medium heat and add rhubarb, water and sugar. Cover and cook for 6 minutes. Remove cover; sprinkle in ginger and cashews. Combine and pour mixture into pie dish. Bake for 60 minutes.

HEALTH BENEFITS
Folk medicine records rhubarb as a purgative and liver cleanser. Chinese medicine promotes the use of rhubarb in clearing 'heat' from the liver, stomach and blood. Cashew nuts have a high iron and vitamin content.

nutri-juices

banana and lime frost zinger

beetroot, celery and apple cleanser

apple, orange and tofu trio

tasty tofu melon shake

rice milk smoothie

blueberry latte

celery, mango and parsley cocktail

nutty nutri-juice

pineapple and mango delight

cranberry cocktail

green goddess

yoghurt skin enhancer

banana and lime frost zinger

Spring into action with this refreshing juice.

SERVES 4

3 ripe bananas, peeled, chopped and frozen
2 cups soymilk
¼ cup ground almonds

1½ limes (finely chopped zest and juice)
Pinch of cinnamon

Place frozen bananas in blender. Add soymilk, almonds, lime zest and juice. Blend until thick and frothy. Sprinkle cinnamon on top.

HEALTH BENEFITS

Ripe bananas provide the body with a good source of energy. Soymilk is lactose-free, non-dairy, rich in calcium and ideal for vegetarians. Cinnamon, an ancient spice, is thought to balance blood-sugar levels.

beetroot, celery and apple cleanser

Looks good; tastes good; makes you feel good.

SERVES 4

1 small fresh beetroot, cut into wedges
1 stalk celery
1 carrot

1 cup fresh apple juice
2 tbsp runny honey

Juice beetroot and set aside. Do the same with celery and carrot. Place apple juice and honey in blender and blend for 30 seconds. Add beetroot, celery and carrot juice. Blend all ingredients until smooth.

HEALTH BENEFITS

Beetroot is an excellent blood cleanser and helps the body fight disease, including cancer. Fresh pineapple juice contains an abundance of vitamins and minerals. Carrots are high in beta-carotene, which the body converts to vitamin A (needed for vision).

clockwise from top left: blueberry latte; pineapple and mango delight; beetroot, celery and apple cleanser; tasty tofu melon shake.

apple, orange and tofu trio

Who would have thought kumara could taste so good in a juice?

SERVES 4

2 apples, peeled and quartered
2 kumara or sweet potatoes, peeled and diced
6 ice cubes
2 cups orange juice

1 cup drained and chopped silken tofu
  (about ¼ block)
1 tsp manuka honey
2 pinches salt

Juice apples and kumara, then place in blender. Add ice, orange juice, tofu, honey and salt. Blend until smooth and frosty. The salt takes away the chalky taste of the tofu.

HEALTH BENEFITS

Oranges contain the vitamin C essential for good bones. They also contain pectin, which is said to help lower 'bad' cholesterol. The zest of the orange contains orange oil. Apples contain antiviral properties, and are known as a cleansing food. Kumara, especially the orange-red variety, are rich in vitamin E and are a good source of iron.

tasty tofu melon shake

Mouth-watering — and silky-smooth thanks to the tofu.

SERVES 4

1 cup crushed ice
1 cup drained and chopped silken tofu
  (about ¼ block)
2 ripe bananas, peeled and sliced

½ tsp vanilla essence
3 cups chopped watermelon
2 tbsp manuka honey
2 pinches salt

Place crushed ice in blender. Add tofu, bananas, vanilla essence, watermelon, honey and salt. Blend until smooth. The salt takes away the chalky tasty of the tofu.

FOOD FOR THOUGHT
For dry skin: whisk 1 egg white, 2 tablespoons manuka honey and 2 teaspoons glycerine together. Fold ¼ cup plain flour in. Apply to face. Rinse off after 20 minutes, then moisturise.

HEALTH BENEFITS
Manuka honey is documented as killing Helicobacter pylori, associated with gastric upsets. Folklore describes honey as being used to treat hay fever. Applied to wounds, it aids healing.

rice milk smoothie

This is a delicious breakfast drink that sets you up for the whole day.

SERVES 4

1 banana, peeled
1 apple, peeled and quartered
2 cups Rice Dream Milk (available from
  health-food stores)

2 tsp manuka honey
1 tsp ginger syrup
1 tbsp LSA meal (ground linseed, sunflower
  and almond seeds)

Juice banana and apple and set aside. Place Rice Dream Milk in blender and add honey, ginger syrup and LSA meal. Blend until smooth and creamy. Add banana and apple juice and blend for a further 30 seconds.

FOOD FOR THOUGHT
Ripe bananas work best in health drinks as they are easier to digest than unripe bananas.

HEALTH BENEFITS
Rice Dream Milk is lactose- and cholesterol-free, as well as low in fat and sodium. It also provides calcium and vitamins A, D and B12. Ginger, famed for its warming properties, stimulates the circulatory system, helps relieve nausea, and fights colds and flu.

blueberry latte

A latte like no other. The combination of fruit, yoghurt and ginger ale produces a light, creamy drink that tastes divine!

SERVES 4

2 small bananas, peeled, chopped and frozen
1 cup café- or creamy latte-flavoured
  yoghurt

1 cup blueberries (fresh, canned or frozen)
1 cup ginger ale
½ cup fruit juice

Place bananas in blender. Add yoghurt, blueberries and ginger ale and blend until creamy. Add ½ cup of your favourite fruit juice. Blend until smooth.

FOOD FOR THOUGHT
If you like smooth, frosty drinks, freeze fruits overnight. Bananas work particularly well in drinks when frozen.

HEALTH BENEFITS
Blueberries help improve circulation and protect blood capillaries. They contain vitamins B and C as well as fibre. Scientists believe that blueberries counteract bacteria that cause urinary tract infections. Folklore often refers to blueberries in relation to the treatment of diarrhoea.

celery, mango and parsley cocktail

A good lunchtime juice that is moreish, to say the least.

SERVES 4

¼ cup parsley
½ stalk celery
1 carrot
1 apple, peeled and quartered

1 cup soymilk
1 cup orange juice
2 large slices mango

Juice parsley, celery, carrot and apple. Set aside. Place soymilk, orange juice and mango in blender. Blend until smooth. Add first juiced mixture to blender. Blend for a further 30 seconds.

FOOD FOR THOUGHT
The outer green stalks of celery are best for making juice.

HEALTH BENEFITS
The exotic mango provides the body with fibre, vitamins E and C, and energy. The fibre in mangoes helps to prevent bowel cancer.

nutty nutri-juice

Nut lovers, this one is definitely for you.

SERVES 4

2 oranges, peeled
3 cups apple juice
1 tbsp wheatgerm
1 tbsp ground almonds

2 tbsp chopped walnuts
1 banana, peeled and sliced
3 tbsp acidophilus yoghurt

Juice oranges and pour juice into blender. Add 1 cup apple juice, wheatgerm, almonds and walnuts. Blend until nuts are well mixed. Add banana and yoghurt and blend until smooth. Slowly add the remaining apple juice. Blend until ingredients are thoroughly combined.

HEALTH BENEFITS

Wheatgerm is high in fibre and brings relief from constipation. Almonds are a good source of calcium and vitamin E. Walnuts contain linoleic acid, which research shows can help to lower cholesterol in the blood.

pineapple and mango delight

Kick-start the day with this easily made juice.

SERVES 4

3 stalks celery
2 carrots
½ cup canned crushed pineapple

½ cup peeled and chopped mango
1 cup apple juice
2 tsp manuka honey

Juice celery and carrots and pour juice into blender. Add pineapple, mango, apple juice and honey. Blend until you have a smooth juice.

HEALTH BENEFITS

Pineapple contains bromelain, which is very kind to the digestive system. Celery helps prevent fluid retention by prompting the elimination processes in the body.

cranberry cocktail

A tasty fruit and vegetable cocktail.

SERVES 4

6 stalks celery
6 ice cubes
1 apple, skin on, cored and chopped
2 plums, peeled, de-stoned and finely diced

1 banana, peeled and sliced
2 cups cranberry juice
1 cup apple juice

Juice celery and set aside. Place ice cubes, apple, plums, banana and cranberry and apple juices into blender. Blend until smooth. Add celery juice and blend for a further 30 seconds.

FOOD FOR THOUGHT
If the fruit you particularly enjoy is out of season, purchase dried fruit and re-hydrate by soaking overnight in a jar or a deep plate filled with water.

HEALTH BENEFITS
Cranberries contain antibiotic properties. They support the body's defence systems and bring relief to women suffering from urinary tract infections that can lead to bladder inflammation or cystitis.

green goddess

Some would say this is not a very pleasant-tasting drink, but it will certainly boost your energy levels.

SERVES 4

3 carrots
2 tbsp finely chopped parsley
2 bananas, peeled and sliced
1 cup finely chopped spinach

1 cup orange juice
2 tsp spirulina powder
2 cups water

Juice carrots and pour juice into blender. Add parsley, bananas and spinach. Blend until smooth. Add orange juice and spirulina and stir well with a spoon. Blend for 1 minute, add water and blend again until spirulina is totally absorbed.

HEALTH BENEFITS
Spinach is rich in iron. Spirulina is often referred to as a 'super food' because it contains chlorophyll and provides the body with more than its daily dose of minerals and vitamins, which will help your skin glow and keep that sparkle in your eyes.

yoghurt skin enhancer

Nourish your skin from within with this delicious smoothie.

SERVES 4

½ cup acidophilus yoghurt
1½ cups trim milk
1 cup orange juice
2 bananas, peeled and sliced

4 dried apricots, finely diced
½ cup peeled and chopped mango
½ tsp manuka honey

Place yoghurt and milk in blender. Add orange juice, bananas, apricots, mango and honey. Blend until smooth and frothy.

FOOD FOR THOUGHT

Yoghurt ice cubes are delicious and make a nice change from ordinary ice cubes. Use in any of this chapter's juices and in smoothies — or give to children to suck.

HEALTH BENEFITS

Yoghurt contains active or live cultures, which bring relief to yeast infections, support the immune system and help the body counteract the side effects of antibiotics.

glossary

BALSAMIC VINEGAR
Rich, dark, slightly sweet Italian vinegar aged in sherry vats.

BREWER'S YEAST
A rich meat alternative. Contains many essential amino acids, B vitamins and minerals.

CHICKPEA AND PEA FLOUR
An excellent alternative to wheat flour; use for fritters and batters in egg-free cooking.

CHINESE GREENS
The best-known of these are bok choy and Chinese cabbage. More enticing and with more vibrant colour (retained in cooking) than European cabbage.

COCONUT FLAKES
Slices of dried coconut, rather than coconut threads or the more common dessicated variety. Roast coconut on purchase for crispness and flavour.

CURRY PASTES
Predominantly Indian or Thai, ready-to-use wet curry pastes range in heat from vindaloo (very hot) to green, red and then yellow paste.

DUKKAH
Middle Eastern spice mix consisting of ground cumin, coriander, sesame seeds and nuts (most commonly hazelnuts).

KÉCAP MANIS
Indonesian sweet soy sauce.

LEMONGRASS
South-East Asian seasoning. Use the white, fat, fleshy end of the stem to cook with, and make tea from the green part of the stem.

LSA MEAL
A mixture of ground linseed, sunflower and almond seeds, available in all good health-food stores.

MISO
Made from fermented soybean mixed with a grain, usually barley or brown rice. It is a multi-purpose savoury seasoning.

MOROCCAN COUSCOUS
Flour-coated semolina. The instant variety takes about 5 minutes to cook.

SESAME SEEDS AND OIL
Roast sesame seeds — and any nuts — as soon as you buy them. This will make them crispy, revitalise their flavour and keep them tasty for longer. Roasted sesame oil, which is dark, is much more flavoursome than plain sesame oil. Roast sesame seeds on a tray in the oven at 170°C until golden-brown.

SOBA NOODLES
Japanese noodles made from the kernel of buckwheat. Eaten hot or cold.

SPANISH PAPRIKA
With the inclusion of chilli, Spanish paprika is spicier than the more traditional Hungarian variety.

STAR ANISE
A brown star-shaped Asian spice, with a liquorice aroma.

TAHINI
Creamed sesame seeds of Lebanese origin.

TAMARI
Japanese-style wheat-free soy sauce.

TEMPEH
Soybean curd, nuttier and coarser in texture than tofu. Must be pan-fried before adding to dish.

TOFU
Bean curd made from soaked and ground soybeans. There are two types, firm and soft-textured (or silken) tofu.

UDON NOODLES
Japanese noodles made from wheat flour. Can be bought fresh or dried.

UMEBOSHI VINEGAR
Japanese plum-flavoured vinegar, drawn from the process of pickling plums.

WASABI POWDER
Made from a Japanese relative of the horseradish family.

WILD RICE
Technically not rice but an aquatic grass. Longer-grain wild rice is the best quality.

index